WHO IS THE HISTORIAN?

WHO IS THE HISTORIAN?

Nigel A. Raab

UNIVERSITY OF TORONTO PRESS

Copyright © University of Toronto Press 2016
Higher Education Division

www.utppublishing.com

Library and Archives Canada Cataloguing in Publication

Raab, Nigel A., 1968–, author
          Who is the historian? / Nigel A. Raab.

Includes bibliographical references and index.

Issued in print and electronic formats.

ISBN 978-1-4426-3573-9 (bound).—ISBN 978-1-4426-3572-2 (paperback).
—ISBN 978-1-4426-3575-3 (pdf).—ISBN 978-1-4426-3574-6 (html).

    1. History—Methodology. 2. Historiography. 3. History—Study and teaching.
4. Historians. I. Title.

D16.R22   2016 907.2   C2015-903596-1

                            C2015-903597-X

We welcome comments and suggestions regarding any aspect of our publications—please feel free to contact us at news@utphighereducation.com or visit our Internet site at www. utppublishing.com.

North America
5201 Dufferin Street
North York, Ontario, Canada, M3H 5T8

2250 Military Road
Tonawanda, New York, USA, 14150

Orders phone: 1-800-565-9523
Orders fax: 1-800-221-9985
Orders e-mail: utpbooks@utpress.utoronto.ca

UK, Ireland, and continental Europe
NBN International
Estover Road, Plymouth, PL6 7PY, UK
orders phone: 44 (0) 1752 202301
orders fax: 44 (0) 1752 202333
orders e-mail: enquiries@nbninternational.com

The University of Toronto Press acknowledges the financial support for its publishing activities of the Government of Canada through the Canada Book Fund.

Printed in the United States of America.

To curiosity

CONTENTS

ACKNOWLEDGMENTS

There is a way in which this book is just one long acknowledgment in recognition of the many individuals—archivists, librarians, and other professionals—who have helped me over the years. Thank you! Colleagues and friends, especially those in the History Department at Loyola Marymount University, provided me with stories about their own experiences in far-flung places. They will certainly be able to recognize the inspiration I gleaned from them. A big thank you to Barret Oliver, a man of many centuries, who let us into his castle on the outskirts of Los Angeles. I also want to thank Natalie Fingerhut at the University of Toronto Press for making timely suggestions and Leanne Rancourt who has done a great job copyediting the manuscript. Finally, thank you Carolyn Peter, my wife and support.

NIGEL A. RAAB
Los Angeles, California

INTRODUCTION

After I had graduated from high school, I followed in the footsteps of my sister and enrolled in the electrical engineering program at Queen's University in Kingston, Ontario. I took all the requisite courses, studied Maxwell's equations, and worked on a thesis project, which tried to send data over phone lines at the same time two people were having a conversation. I received respectable grades, got my degree, and landed a rather plum job in Switzerland. I was well paid, had intelligent colleagues, and could look forward to a rewarding career at a major international corporation.

Something was missing, though. Throughout my years at Queen's, we engineers poked fun at the artsies and had unprintable slogans to describe their endeavors. Despite the banter, I could never commit myself. While doing the thesis project (whose subject matter had not been my idea), my focus wandered off and I spent more time with electives in the history department than in the laboratory soldering capacitors and inductors into an electronic circuit. I discovered that the complexity of the electronic circuit was nothing compared to the complexity of human experience; the sheer variety of human situations I discovered in my history courses took control of my imagination. Limitless paths opened up before me as I explored the fates of national communities, individual villagers, industrial workers, talented women, and every possible combination of the above. I could not get a history degree based just on these electives, so I decided to work as an engineer only until I had saved up enough money to study history.

When I returned to the history books, I had a narrow vision of the path I wanted to pursue. I was completely focused on completing a PhD and becoming a history professor, since these instructors and researchers had been my role models as an undergraduate. With the Cold War nearing an end, Russian history was still very much in vogue and the exploits of the mid-nineteenth-century revolutionaries captured the hearts of young men like myself. At a basic level, the Canadian in me was also interested in studying a country that was big and cold—this has turned out to be enormously helpful because every time I travel to Moscow, St. Petersburg, Kazan, or Kiev in Ukraine I feel perfectly at home with the climate, thus making my research that much easier. I took courses on revolution in which the world was always being turned upside down—this was exciting stuff for a wandering soul. Once the path had been selected, I made sure I stuck to it: I finished an undergraduate degree at Queen's, did a master's at the University of Zurich, and then completed my PhD in Russian history at Columbia University in New York City.

The transition I made over 20 years ago has been rewarded over and over again. I have been able to study volunteer associations in nineteenth-century Russia, the social response to disasters in the Soviet Union, and the emergence of photography in the Russian Empire. I have been fortunate enough to speak on the radio, attend conferences in Germany, and develop courses with intellectual content that reflects my own specific interests yet intersects with important societal trends—I recently taught a course on the "History of Walking" as an attempt to turn a mundane activity into a subject for historical analysis. Outside the research, I have had interesting interactions with cultural attachés, journalists, state department officials, filmmakers, and lawyers who understand Russian law well enough to advise American companies doing business in the Russian Federation.

The transition served me well, but through conversations with students over the years I have learned two important things. First, not everyone interested in history wants to pursue a doctorate and become a history professor, thus many individuals are not quite sure what can be done with a history degree. Of course, the word *history* in the last sentence could be replaced with *English* or *philosophy* or *humanities*. At some level, this discovery was a little shocking—what could be more exciting than revealing all the complex layers of what it is to be you and me? Second, I learned of a problem of which I was a part. I had benefited so much from a degree in the humanities, yet I was not conveying these opportunities to students in a meaningful way. Yes, they were learning about the centralization of power under Ivan the Terrible, certainly an important insight given the resurgence of Russia under Putin, but this is still just academic learning. I was conveying information without suggesting why someone would enjoy collecting all this information. Although history professors and their kin are not career counselors, I realized our students had a hard time translating a factoid about sixteenth-century Russia into a meaningful component of a life well lived after graduation. What opportunities were available to graduates of history, in particular, and the humanities, in general?

Two gaps therefore had to be filled. First, the historian has to be more than the invisible figure who writes books or assists television programs with accuracy. Who is the historian? Who is the person who assembles historical information and uses the information to argue a point about the past? In a sense, I am fleshing out the author's name from the inside cover of a book and letting that name grow into a three-dimensional figure.

The professional historian spends countless hours poring over old documents, discovering long-forgotten texts, and interpreting the meaning of artifacts. Yet the excitement of the historical profession cannot be limited to the discovery of a factoid here and there because this limits the historical profession to academic and intellectual exercises. The historian is a physical being who does physical activities that cannot all be subsumed into the proverbial life of the mind. A generation ago the historian conjured images of a quiet man, young or old, who had worn holes in the elbows of his tweed jacket because he had been sitting at a library desk for far too long. The image of the historian in a tweed jacket had parallels with the medical doctor in the white overcoat. Just as the white overcoat separated the doctor from mere mortals, the tweed was a mark of the higher mind. Nowadays, the tweed jackets have largely disappeared, but a lack of clarity about the historian persists. Who is the historian, and what does he or she do?

Second, the word *historian* is too often associated with academic historians who work in the history departments of major universities. This association marginalizes individuals who employ a historical education in other environments and makes it more difficult for creative young individuals to envision where the historical road might take them. This is perhaps a principal reason that alternate roads have been so difficult to conceptualize. In this instance the question has to be modified a little: Who is the historian when we look beyond academic departments? No single chapter of this book is entirely focused on this question, but each chapter slowly introduces kindred spirits whose job titles may not include the word *historian* but whose activities are historical indeed. With each step along the way, the second gap will shrink as readers are pulled outside history departments to experience historical thinking in a broader world.

This is not a frivolous exercise. Increasingly, history and the humanities have become targeted by university administrators obsessed in measurable statistical returns and by parents who just want a steady job for their children. Fearful lest their bright daughter with a history degree become a dog walker in Central Park, they ease and nudge her into safer fields such as business or economics. In an age that is dazzled by technologies and the monthly payments technological devices require, scientifically inclined fields have become the darlings at our universities.

The weakness of this scientific position is treated as self-evident throughout the humanities, but history and humanities departments have been less than effective at promoting their interests. All too often we fall back on traditional explanations that no longer stir people to action. We spread the word that "critical thinking" builds a "well rounded person," yet we seem to have been saying this for centuries. If historical analysis teaches us to look for differences rather than similarities, a new approach is absolutely necessary. A positive platform that adds a degree of physicality to historical pursuits can only help to invigorate the discipline in a time of crisis.

A select few may worry that the life of the mind will be in jeopardy— that the contemplative pursuit of the academic will succumb to physical and vocational pressures. But this fear is ill conceived since historians have always moved in public places in one form or another. The late Eric Hobsbawm understated his own physical commitment to the lived environment when he wrote in the preface to *Primitive Rebels* that "[s]ome personal contact, however slight, with the people and even the places about which the historian writes, is essential if he is to understand problems which are exceedingly remote from the normal life of the British university teacher." The physical environment does not have to be rebellious to be interesting, as the examples below readily show. Highlighting all of these physical spaces simply brings standard practice to the fore to fill a void in our understanding of the historian, however broadly we define this individual. Let us not worry, then, and instead move forward as we promote the past.

At one time or another, we have all been fascinated by a work about history. Perhaps we read a history of Napoleon or a history of the French Revolution or even a history of sex in the Middle Ages. These books, however, arrive on our desks in polished form and obscure the process through which the book was made. The experience is similar to watching a film where we quickly lose sight of all the takes, retakes, and editing in the process. With the arrival of DVDs, film studios give glimpses into the behind-the-scenes activities with "the making of" clips that viewers can watch. Books rarely have a "making of" section, so it is difficult to understand the lengthy process that leads to the physical book.

Unlike a film industry designed to foster public consumption, professional historians rarely target large audiences. In return, the public has questioned the reclusive position of scholars who have isolated themselves from the public eye. The general reader only experiences the scholar transubstantiated into a book without seeing the process behind that book. A historian can claim that she dedicated 10 years of her life to the book, but we don't understand what went on in those 10 years. Unfortunately, when we only see the finished product our fascination for the past is limited to the actions and events of the past and we thus overlook the exciting dynamics of the historical profession. It is certainly intriguing to learn that Isaac Newton studied alchemy, but it would be equally exciting to understand the route through which historians brought this information to our attention.

Unfortunately, very few works are available that adequately bring the historical profession to life. Many earnest tomes have discussed the methodology of the historian, problems of historical periodization, and the importance of abstract theory to the historian's work. There are a few exceptions, such as *The Historian's Craft* by Marc Bloch, but the majority of the books that examine the work of the historian are devoted to the intellectual rather than the lived experience of the historian. The reader will learn about the evaluation of documents, but not about the complex process through which the historian discovered those documents and the particular circumstances in which those documents were read. Similarly, methodological books rarely pay attention to the working partners of academics. Since it is attractive to present intellectual activities as a function of a brilliant mind, the co-workers in these enterprises are often overlooked. The historian, however, works together with a host of collaborators who supply additional spice to the project. By focusing on the real physical environment of the professional historian, we will gain a much better appreciation of how fulfilling this calling can be.

If we take the time to look inside the world of the historian, we discover a dynamic profession. The historian can't rip off the tweed jacket to reveal a suit of armor underneath, but the pursuit of the past requires a bit of audacity. A historian can fly to Paris to work underground at the Bibliothèque Nationale de France—François Mitterrand or find a desk 10 stories high at the Robarts Library in Toronto. If European and North American reading rooms still lack luster, the historian can take a seat in tropical reading rooms in Cuba or in the rainy cities of New Zealand. In his wonderfully researched work on the environmental attitudes of imperial powers, Richard Grove and his assistants visited archives on islands and in cities around the world. Bibliographies in books don't often read like tour guides, but in Grove's work the locations of the libraries and archives draw the reader on a world tour— Kalkuta, Bangalore, New Delhi, Mauritius, Cape Town, Trinidad and Tobago, Edinburgh, St. Vincent and the Grenadines.

Whether on the island of Mauritius in the Indian Ocean or in the city of Paris in France, the historian moves around physical spaces. It is not an abstract historian working in a stereotypical library but a real historian encountering strange and compelling environments en route. All too often these experiences are polished out of published works even though they represent an essential part of the process. An American historian in Paris can develop a headache from the excess of wine he drank the night before, whereas a Russian historian in Mauritius can be so overwhelmed by the wonderful weather she never gets down to business.

At a very minimum, historians are travelers and wanderers. Herodotus, the Greek historian who wrote almost 500 years before the birth of Christ, traveled around the Mediterranean and the Black Sea to collect his mix of facts and fancies. He did not visit archives but, deeply interested in the past, he collected stories and rumors and wove this information into his histories. In this spirit, modern historians extend their carbon footprint by flying to the four corners of the globe. Forrest McDonald traveled 70,000 miles in a dilapidated Plymouth to collect material for his work on the economic origins of the American constitution. Every city of the world has numerous historical depositories spread throughout its neighborhoods. A historian in Los Angeles can hop in the car, drive through a series of ethnic neighborhoods (a world tour of its own), pass a couple of strip malls and recycling centers, and land at a library that holds invaluable documents about the immigrant experience in the United States.

These physical aspects form the basis for the first chapter, "The Spaces in Which We Work." The two main protagonists in this chapter are the archive and the library. No two archives or two libraries are, however, alike. One archive can have an armed guard at the entrance, whereas another archive allows anyone to pass through the door. One archive can be organized upon rigid scientific principles whereas another can be organized by local volunteers. Whether in St. Petersburg, San Francisco, Paris, or Toronto, libraries fill different roles, provide different materials, and offer unique physical environments for studying the past. From labyrinthine structures to open atriums, the working space shifts radically. Libraries and archives are not the only spaces a historian has occasion to visit; they are, however, the two most common places.

The attention given to these physical spaces reflects contemporary shifts in research as well. Over the years historians have developed more sensitivity to spatial issues. Whereas a historian researching in 1950 could write about diplomatic issues of the Napoleonic Wars without considering the space in which the discussions transpired, contemporary historians pay greater attention to the rites and rituals of these important political processes: What room did the discussion take place in? What were the participants wearing? What gifts were exchanged?

In the second chapter, "The Sources We Use," we explore the physical evidence that is gathered from physical spaces. Even when we think we have direct evidence, sources have complex levels of meaning that must be taken into consideration. Any text, object, or speck of evidence from the past qualifies as a source. Philosophically, one might even say that once the item is no longer in the immediate now, it is fair game for the historian. The sheer volume of sources can, however, be approached and organized in a meaningful way. For historians who work in the modern period, written sources tend to dominate. The rise of the modern state in the seventeenth century produced a new form of political organization and new bureaucracies that issued a growing paper trail. In addition to this bureaucratic information, historians have used diaries, memoirs, newspapers, and the like to interpret the past.

In the last generation, visual and aural sources have become more important. As a reaction to film and photography and as a reflection of the visual experience of the Internet, historians have become more careful about visual interpretations of the world. The methodology is not entirely new since art historians have been visual practitioners for centuries and musicologists have studied treble clefs for an equally long time. Yet this expertise, previously housed in specific historical subdisciplines, now flows into general studies. Historians are receptive to photographs and moving images as components of historical investigations. Sound profiles in physical environments have gained less attention, but these sounds are slowly emerging as important sources in their own right. These seemingly peculiar sources transform even the most straightforward situation and can be interpreted and diversified in exciting ways.

If historians have paid greater attention to a physical environment, it is not unjustified to pay greater attention to the individuals who work in places such as libraries and archives, for historians rely upon a web of professionals. To highlight these interactions, the third chapter, "The Web of the Historian's Work," explores how the historian's interactions with these professionals can shape the research process. Each library has a staff of trained professionals, and each archive has a team of cataloguers, conservators, and collectors. In order to conduct meaningful research, the historian needs to start conversations with these librarians, archivists, and curators; this activity represents a substantial component of the day-to-day activity of historical research. A conversation with a librarian can trigger a chain reaction that inspires a network of further conversations.

Historians require these contacts to gain access to as diverse a source base as possible. In the not-so-distant past, the historian could be satisfied with the memoirs of a famous general. Today, however, a seemingly endless array of sources has become available. This multiplies interpretive possibilities, but it also makes the historian more dependent on external expertise to find these sources. With a curator of a natural history museum, the historian can ask questions about food supplies in a region of interest. With an archivist, the historian can inquire into the acquisition or organization of materials that had previously been in private hands. A discussion with an employee at a film studio can bring to light dusty reels of film that store clues about the past.

This chapter also looks at the academic friends of the historian to ensure that traditional aspects of the enterprise don't get lost. If historians travel the physical world, they also travel the academic world and freely draw ideas from across campus. A traditional historian might limit himself to his peers and take books off the shelf to gently add an additional perspective. For example, an environmental history of Germany can be enhanced if it adds a comparative perspective with environmental issues in France. More recently, the emphasis has been placed on cooperative research with nontraditional partners—from science, literature, and philosophy, to name a few. To address this shift in thinking, the end of Chapter 3 looks at historians who have dipped into other disciplines. John Komlos employed anthropometrics and gathered data about the height of soldiers to draw conclusions about health; William McNeill studied biological phenomena associated with microparasites to reinterpret the European conquest of the New World; Paul Veyne employed contemporary French philosophy to reassess how the Greeks approached their myths.

The interdisciplinary movement gained momentum well before the age of the Internet, so scholars could not predict the influence of digital technologies on historical research even though the Internet necessarily adds an interdisciplinary element to research. In fact, as our attention turns to digital issues in the fourth chapter, "The Historian in the Digital Age," the Internet both embodies and challenges the themes presented in the first three chapters. On the one hand, it returns the historian to her office since the availability of digital sources makes certain trips to archives redundant. On the other hand, it radically complicates the notion of sources—in the past, historians did not have to consider sources that were not only continually changing but also radically different depending on who accessed them. Unlike archival materials, web content continues to change. A webpage can be here today and gone tomorrow, and the content of the webpage, ads and all, depends on the profile of the user who accessed it. Whereas in the past a historian could assume that the writer and recipient of a letter had the same document in their hands, this is no longer true with email since the visual reading context has become personalized.

With the Internet, information has become more readily available and new information is produced at a heretofore unseen rate. Google estimates that every two days we create as much information as we did from the dawn of history until 2003. With this massive production of data, historians should already start to think about how their colleagues in the year 2115 will be accessing historical information and conducting their research—will young historians in the year 2115 be so overwhelmed by the amount of available information that they simply give up on the past? The tools required to search an archive are not the same as the tools required to search Google, where mathematical algorithms steer the user. Chapter 4 explores the issues future historians will face as they are confronted with such a mass of seemingly unmanageable data.

The journey from the dull scholar in a tweed jacket to the globetrotting persona and web-surfing researcher risks exaggerating the role of the historian, but it has the benefit of transforming two-dimensional writing into the cultural production of a living human being. It acts as a corrective to a misperceived isolation and places the historian within a huge communications network characterized by sharing, cooperation, and the exchange of ideas. The dynamic activities that surround historical research might even bear an element of fun.

If the first four chapters of this book portray the historical profession in dynamic terms, the last two chapters focus on becoming both a historian and an individual who benefits from understanding historical practice. When we read works of professional historians we tend to forget that they went through the same undergraduate training as the journalist or cultural attaché. The road to becoming a historian is an arduous but enjoyable task. Although we often take writing for granted, the young historian has to continually hone his writing and research skills. Sloppiness in writing often leads to sloppiness in thought. Crafting careful sentences, introducing the appropriate metaphors, and polishing transitions from one paragraph to the next can be perceived as tedious exercises, but they are keys to clarity and improve communication with any potential audience. While some maintain that history is in the past and therefore does not change, interpretations of the past change with regularity. Keen minds do not study history to memorize dates or to list key events (this is especially true in a digital age when the facts of the matter can be easily googled). Rather, the young historian is trained to listen for unexpected sounds and seek out the significance of historical trends: What is the relationship between causes and consequences? Which social groups have been marginalized? What forces led to globalization in the preindustrial age? This style of questioning leads to limitless possibilities. When the answers are presented in accessible prose, the historian has an opportunity to convey important viewpoints—on politics, race, gender issues, nationalism—to a broad audience.

Therefore, the history student has to pay careful attention to shifting interpretations and understand how to merge these interpretations with newly acquired primary sources. Not everyone who knows something about the past, collects artifacts from a specific historical epoch, or watches the History Channel is a historian. The awareness of past events must be attached to a sophisticated skill set embodied through research and interpretation. The task is not easy, especially if one wishes to pursue a doctoral dissertation, but the rewards are immense. Anyone who opens her mind in this fashion will be open to the world.

Without promoting a course curriculum, the fifth chapter, "The Skill Set of the Historian," says a few words about historical training. How can one promote critical explorations to prepare a historian to become a cosmopolitan citizen in a digital world? What skills will make the student of history able to move easily between the world of historical research and the world of practical decision making? It might seem strange to begin with the trained professional and end with the younger generation, yet placing these questions toward the end of this book introduces a platform to explore future directions for the historical profession.

In seeking new directions, "History, the Historian, and the Humanities," the final chapter in this book and an invitation to a larger public discussion, debates the role of the historical profession in today's cultural and political climate. History and similar disciplines in the humanities have been the target of budget cuts and criticism for their limited worth in the contemporary world. Criticized for a focus on abstract theory and accused of being economically inefficient in a competitive marketplace, historians have been forced to defend their activities. It is awkward for such an eminently dynamic profession to defend itself, but such has been the mood over the last decade or so. Let us then look at the more substantial criticisms aimed at historians and see how well they fare when paired with the knowledge we have gained from the preceding chapters. When we understand the historian in a physical world of archives, libraries, sounds, moving images, open-air museums, and ideas, we can reposition the historian and highlight the important role both history and the historian play in the three-dimensional contemporary world.

Chapter 1

THE SPACES IN WHICH
WE WORK

In 1989, Scott Adams published the first *Dilbert* cartoon to satirize the office environment. Adams's cartoon brought the office cubicle into the mainstream and provided a glimpse into the inglorious physical environment of nondescript office buildings. The cartoon is poking fun at a bureaucratic environment, but many historians have offices no larger than cubicles.

Just the same, the four walls of the office don't define the professional workspace. The historian travels to archives, libraries, museums, galleries, and outdoor sites to collect information about the past; it is only with great difficulty that we can limit the office space of the historian. This phenomenon is familiar to other professions as well. A doctor has an office but also has responsibilities in the emergency department; a lawyer has an office but visits the courtroom for extensive stays; a farmer has an office but wanders through field and forest in the open air.

Unfortunately, these various work locations remain mysterious to many readers. Archives are the depositories of hard, physical evidence, yet few people know what an archive looks like. An archive can be concealed in an eighteenth-century palace or a contemporary highrise. In three minutes on an urban street in downtown Moscow, a pedestrian can stroll past the complete collection of state documents from three centuries of Russian and Soviet history and not even know it. In Moscow, Los Angeles, San Francisco, Austin, Paris, and beyond, large buildings hold millions of documents. Libraries and museums are more conspicuous with their daring architecture, but even then few people walk through them and even fewer have an opportunity to explore the guts of these institutions. As a corrective, let us take this opportunity to travel far and wide into archives and libraries to explore them as physical spaces.

In a country with such a centralized tradition of governance, it should come as no surprise that the Russian capital has the biggest bounty of historical documents. Moscow certainly has countless archives, but the State Archive of the Russian Federation, known by its Russian acronym GARF, dominates its smaller cousins. Yet GARF, which is situated in the heart of downtown Moscow and occupies the equivalent of a city block, is only recognizable from a small plaque on the wall. If you stand at the corner of the nearest Metro station and ask a local to point the way to the archive, more than likely you will receive a blank look.

Perhaps the archive is seemingly unnoticeable because state documents are associated with state secrets; why bother with such an unsavory institution? To be sure, the archive was a sensitive place in the Soviet era, and researchers found plenty of *sekretno* in the finding aids, indicating that these files were out of reach for readers. Scores of these files became available after the collapse of the Soviet Union in 1991, but this did not mean that the archive became a more hospitable place. In the middle of the turbulent 1990s, the state positioned guards armed with automatic weapons just outside the reading room. It took a little courage to walk by the muzzles of what one could only assume were loaded guns. Theoretically, the archive was open to anyone as long as he could demonstrate affiliation with an educational institution or a need to trace familial information. Practically, however, the presence of the guards often gave readers second thoughts about entering. Nowadays visitors can get their feet wet by first visiting the archival website (www.statearchive.ru) and then walking into the physical archive.

The actual collection in GARF is vast but off limits to readers. Of the entire city block, visitors only see a small reading room. The reading room, perhaps twice the size of a high school classroom, has 40 or so desks arranged in a grid pattern. The room is bare and functional without unnecessary distractions; occasionally one hears a car alarm from the street below. If so desired, the reader can tell time by looking through the large windows at the end of the reading room. In the heart of winter, the setting sun at mid-afternoon gives a concrete sense that closing time is approaching. However one checks the time, it just slips away as one leafs through stories about mining disasters in the 1960s, power outages in the 1950s, famine in the 1930s, and the wide array of random events that fill the pages of these documents.

Even the most conscientious archival researcher will take a look at other laborers in the room. When you glance around, you quickly realize that you don't know why the other readers are there—what is that man sitting to my right interested in? You can naively assume that they are all writing dissertations but, if you ask, you get varied answers: the keeper of a small Siberian museum had arrived to collect information and photographs about an exile soon to be featured in a local exhibit; an assistant from a Russian state ministry had come to find anecdotes for a short public relations piece the ministry was putting together; an Armenian hoped to discover information about Armenian politicians who had been particularly active during *perestroika* (Mikhail Gorbachev's program to reform the communist system in the 1980s). Every individual in the room invents the archive anew.

The institutional setting should not obscure the deeply personal reasons for sitting in the reading room. After the collapse of the Soviet Union, visitors sought the truth about oppressive episodes in Soviet history. At a more intimate level, individuals arrived at the archives to research the fate of their ancestors. Family members desperately wanted to know why a grandparent had disappeared, and in the quiet of the archive, where talking is essentially forbidden, the occasional sob broke the silence as the documents revealed the brutal truth to surviving family members.

Archives are normally considered heartless spaces because we associate them with state bureaucracies and large institutions. A little official plaque that advertises the archive won't do anything to alter this stereotype. In contrast, smaller archives can be less intimidating in no small part because of their curb appeal. The Southern California Library for Social Studies and Research in Los Angeles has outdoor walls painted with a colorful mural that reflects its mission. The images of expressive faces of immigrants and workers link the archive with the emotional fates of the surrounding community. While the mural, an archival document in its own right, may appear less intimidating than a ministerial plaque, it nevertheless carries a strong message about the struggles and fights of minority groups in Los Angeles.

The Southern California Library has an interesting history, beginning with its location. If many archives have privileged locations in the center of town, the Southern California Library is in South Los Angeles, an area known for its social and economic problems. The building sits on a busy but very pedestrian street, a stone's throw from the epicenter of the LA riots that took place in the early 1990s. Fifty years ago, left-leaning intellectuals opened the library and made it a depository for their materials. During the Red Scare shortly after World War II, it became a safe haven for incriminating materials that otherwise might have been discovered in their homes. The library therefore has an extensive collection of personal papers from that era as well as a vast collection of books about Marx, Lenin, Trotsky, and the global communist movement. The boxes in the back contain old Soviet journals, and the magazine shelf has journals produced by labor movements in Switzerland and elsewhere.

The original mission of the library has been modified over the years, both in terms of its position as a depository of documents and the issues it promotes. In pedestrian streets, residents observe who comes and goes from the buildings. In the case of the Southern California Library, onlookers watched as white people—traditional Marxist intellectuals—walked in and out of the door. In a predominantly African-American neighborhood, the address became identified with the interests of an alien group. Just by seeing people enter and exit, the space became defined as a foreign and strange space and as a place that was "not for us"—the doors of the library were open to all, but not everyone felt comfortable going in. Over the years, however, the library has made efforts to attract residents who live in the neighborhood. It now organizes historical walking tours so local youth become invested in the past, present, and future of the neighborhood in which they live.

The desire to reach out to the neighborhood has consequences directly related to archival practices. Archival science has become an increasingly complex discipline, and over the last century archives have made the transition from being Byzantine structures in which no one except the archivist knew where documents were to being scientific structures in which no one except the archivist knows where documents are; universities now offer courses in archival science. Yet an overtly scientific ordering of documents, certainly a necessity in many instances, can alienate timid users. In an effort to overcome another barrier, the Southern California Library has sought neighborhood participation in ordering and cataloguing the collection. The active participation exposes the untrained archivist to documents they might otherwise never see. Furthermore, by sitting in the archival–library space they become linked to that space. This solves the problem that the archive holds thousands of stories about the African-American experience in Los Angeles, yet many African-American inhabitants hesitate to explore those stories. The creative methods of archiving make the space user friendly to the users who matter most.

In contrast to many archives, the Southern California Library is open access—that is, you can walk in, sit down, and use the materials. It does not require a letter or attestation; in the spirit of the Marxist intellectuals who founded the library, individuals outside the traditional intellectual classes do not face barriers when trying to learn about class history. The Huntington Library, only 28 kilometers away, offers a sharp contrast in admission standards. If you are faculty at a university and have a PhD in your proposed field of research, then you can send in an online application. If you do not fulfill the above qualifications, then you need two letters of recommendation and you cannot submit the application electronically. Substantial hurdles face a user outside of mainstream academic life at the Huntington Library.

The varying difficulty in access reflects attitudes toward the materials themselves. The Huntington Library possesses a complete Gutenberg Bible; such a rarity requires careful preservation. In contrast, the Southern California Library places emphasis on consumption rather than preservation. The materials are to be touched and experienced as physical objects. If they should wear out through usage all the better, since this testifies that their meaning has been passed on from generation to generation. This is not to say that the Southern California Library is indifferent to preservation since it has rescued important materials from the dumpster, but that the emphasis is placed elsewhere.

If the Southern California Library is innovative because the atmosphere encourages local participation, it also invites historians from other parts of town to experience a neighborhood and archival environment they might not typically see. Josh Sides, now a noted historian of California, describes his first experiences of the neighborhood as inspirational in his life and career. When he arrived at the library just after the LA riots of 1992, the neighborhood had a "funereal" atmosphere—buildings around the library had been burned to the ground. As a white person, he recognized his status as an outsider, especially since groups of African-American men referred to him as "blue" (i.e., an undercover police officer). Yet the desolate street atmosphere changed the moment he entered the library where volunteers were busily cataloguing and documenting the materials. The contrast between the outside and the inside was an integral part of working in the archive.

Our working lives are full of small transitional moments that we rarely perceive as such—walking up or down a staircase, entering or exiting a room, driving in or out of a tunnel. These moments influence our perceptions of the places where we work. Sides describes an uncomfortable sensation on the street but a warmth once he was inside the library. The library had a familiar feeling and thus offered what can effectively be considered a protective sanctuary. A resident might feel more comfortable on the street and hesitate before entering the library because it was a foreign space. Since the meaning of the two physical spaces has been reversed, we get a much better understanding of how the physical space of the archive affects our search for knowledge. Unlike Sides, many researchers choose their documents from more familiar locations, therefore influencing the outcome of their research.

In contrast to the Southern California Library, the City Archives of Cologne, Germany, attracts historians because of its collection and central location in a beautiful city. Dating back to the fourteenth century, the archive is one of the oldest in Europe. Originally placed in a chest, it quickly expanded and became the depository for all city-related matters. City officials stored the meeting protocols, communications with other cities, and letters to princes and lords in the area. It now contains over 65,000 documents on parchment, over a million photographs, and countless personal collections of important German cultural figures. Having managed to survive World War II, the archive remained a central depository for documents. In 1971, as the archive continued to grow, the current building was constructed to accommodate approximately 30 kilometers of shelf length.

But even the best-laid plans for a comfortable research trip in a peaceful area can be undone. Such was the case for many researchers on 3 March 2009. When readers entered the building at the start of the day, few were expecting that they would have to flee the building before it collapsed. At about two in the afternoon, construction workers found a water leak and notified the building authorities. Later that day, the building collapsed because the construction of subway tunnels had loosened the earth (even before the collapse authorities had noticed that the archive had sunk about

20 millimeters). Fortunately, the archival staff and individuals in the reading room escaped just in time, though the crash caused fatalities in a neighboring structure.

Once it was clear that no one had life-threatening injuries in the building, the attention turned to the collection. Historians and archivists were shocked at the possibility that invaluable books and manuscripts could be lost forever; the fear was heightened by forecasts for rain. In good German fashion, the rescue of the manuscripts got underway almost immediately. The archival staff, the local fire department, volunteers, and historians pitched in to save what were effectively the materials they wanted to read once the building had been restored. In conversation with a German historian, I discovered his sense of amazement at handling these muddy treasures. Works that he had normally touched with the utmost delicacy had been tossed around pell-mell and exposed to the most hazardous of conditions. Fortunately, the archive managed to save the majority of its collection.

The rescue of documents in Cologne presents an example of well-organized German archivists (versus their rather sloppy counterparts in structural engineering). German archivists were, however, not always interested in rescuing ancient German documents. After the Nazi invasion of France, the Nazis sent in trained archivists to gather key materials (such as the original Treaty of Versailles) and send them back to Berlin where they could be analyzed. As much as 140 tons of military documents made their way back to special archives in or around the German capital. To complicate matters, once the Soviet army entered Germany, it sent in its own archival experts who had the materials shipped back to Moscow. After the war, the French government had to negotiate with the Soviets to see materials that were originally stolen by the Germans.

This type of movement of archival materials complicates life for the historian because she does not always know where the documents are, and even if the location is known, getting permission to look at these "stolen" or "saved" documents can be complicated. Fortunately, historians and archivists work together on this issue in an effort to trace the movement of files. Patricia Kennedy Grimsted has worked for decades visiting archives all over Europe. In her effort to catalogue the whereabouts of archival documents and publicize the plight of millions of rare German books rotting in a church north of Moscow, she made it possible for researchers to access materials in danger of disappearing. Beyond the practical question of research, this work has also led to the development of international agreements on the restitution of files. Much like the return of stolen art, the return of archival documents has a controversial legal dimension that requires international agreements. Grimsted takes her readers through the maze of intrigue and exposes them to castles, churches, and other unexpected depositories of major collections.

Evidently, one does not always have to visit a formal institution to gather research materials. For example, the discovery of an archive can begin with a telephone call. There is a story of an elderly woman from Poughkeepsie, New York, who phoned a museum at Cornell University and told them that the photographs of her aunt's lover had been saved from the garbage heap. Her aunt's lover was Herbert B. Turner, a well-respected photographer, world traveler, and publishing tycoon from Boston at the start of the twentieth century. He had taken pictorialist images of Gloucester, Massachusetts; New York City; and Venice, Italy. When he died in 1937, his obituary referred to him as a photographer of kings, emperors, and princes throughout the world. The aunt's niece believed the images were worth preserving.

The curator–historian who was assigned to explore the collection was unable to decide what to do based on the phone call and instead drove across upstate New York to visit Poughkeepsie. Once there she was led into the basement to sift through old photographs. A basement in upstate New York does not have the facilities of a reading room, and only instinct can help a researcher navigate through the materials under these circumstances. Here excitement is paired with nervous energy—the optimist sees herself on the edge of a major discovery while the pessimist feels that because she cannot possibly look at everything she risks failure by overlooking something. Unable to finish the task the same day, the hostess invited the curator to stay the night and continue in the morning. Although the museum ultimately declined the photographs, the historian had an exciting adventure in an unexpected work environment.

In even stranger circumstances a historian can sometimes be invited to review historical materials about themselves. The work environment remains that of the formal institution, but the personal materials embed historians in their own past. It is still difficult to determine how much material the American government collects on scholars, but much is now known about Soviet and communist practices. American scholars visiting the Eastern Bloc in the 1970s and 1980s could expect the local secret police to cast an eye on their activities. Through information collected by informers and tapping devices, the secret police collected thousands of pages of personal information. After the Berlin Wall came down, researchers were allowed to look at their own files. The archival information created an awkward and at times unpleasant trip down memory lane; the secret police had essentially written their biographies. Photographs of forgotten friends and accounts of intimate dinners revived memories of bygone times. In contrast to many archival experiences, the historians in these circumstances were not being exposed to someone else's experience.

The decision to preserve these personal files well after the end of the communist era parallels the niece's desire to preserve the work of a distant relative. Importantly, and this was true in Poughkeepsie, photographs and other antiques are not always accepted into collections. An archive has limited space, a professional staff has to process the additions, and every acquisition draws on a finite supply of resources. As a consequence, interesting remnants of the past disappear even though they had, in the case of the basement in Poughkeepsie, been saved from the dustbin of history. But how much should be saved? Would historians be better off if every farm implement from the nineteenth century had been preserved? Are we any worse for wear because the majority of Charles Dickens's novels purchased in nineteenth-century bookstores have long since been incinerated or composted? Similarly, documentation known to archival experts can disappear for the understandable reason that it is impossible for an archivist to collect everything, even if the archive has much more space than a basement in Poughkeepsie.

Archives are, in general, organized places, but readers receive material in random forms. An archive can contain paper files, microfiche, photographs, film canisters, and larger objects such as clothing or vases. In the case of files, you might receive little more than a stack of papers and you cannot anticipate what the file will contain; it therefore takes patience to search for the needle in that haystack. Libraries, on the other hand, are now designed to have a welcoming feel and present information in a nicely published format. At libraries, the books have already gone through an added stage of editing (such as the publication in book form of personal letters assembled from an archival collection) and thus meet the user in a more accessible form. The wide open stacks of the library filled with published volumes fill a different need than the archive, where the archivists organize government papers, boxes of personal writing, and random documents. The added level of organization at the library can give the impression that the archives are more exciting because they hold greater mystery in those dusty old pages. Yet the ordered rows of books only tell a small part of the story: Library environments draw the historian into fascinating spaces. If users of an archive never see more than a small reading room, the library has aisles upon aisles of books and doors leading hither and thither. Throughout the quiet space, magic whispers encourage exploration.

Older libraries are spellbinding because of their labyrinthine qualities. Modern tourists from the United States who travel to Italian cities are fascinated by the twists and turns of medieval streets; they visit them precisely because they offer a refreshing change from the grid patterns of America's modern cities. Similarly, getting lost in a library is part of the fun. Who has not enjoyed entering the Butler Library at Columbia University to discover that the perimeter of the building has full floors whereas the stacks in the core of the building are divided into half floors? Strange stairways take the browser from one half floor to the next. Other libraries have perfectly normal elevators without divided stairs but have rooms far off the beaten path. Each library has as many idiosyncrasies as the medieval city.

In St. Petersburg, the Russian National Library has its origins at the end of the eighteenth century, a latecomer by European standards. Catherine the Great, the enlightened empress from Germany, gave permission to construct the first Imperial Russian Public Library. At the start of the nineteenth century, the library was a grandiose building in the center of town, though it is now overwhelmed by car traffic on the Nevsky Prospekt. You can, however, still walk into the building through imposing doors and enter into the eighteenth century. The foyer is modest and unassuming, but don't be fooled. You will quickly and cheerfully get lost as you wander down half-lit corridors with ancient busts and portraits of Russian luminaries. Every few steps a large door with a little plaque signals a hidden treasure. If you do not go in, just imagine what lies behind.

I did have to enter one room to read journals on fires in peasant communes. When I first walked in I experienced standard fare—I heard the light sound of fluttering paper as scores of readers earnestly turned pages of journals from more than two centuries of Russian history. But it got interesting once I asked for a journal that they could not release into the reading room. When I submitted a request slip for an illustrated weekly from the 1890s, the librarian told me to follow her. I did so with hesitation.

I walked around the librarian's desk and passed old wooden bookshelves sagging under ponderous books covered in weightless dust. The librarian urged me to duck under an antiquated book retrieval system that resembled a miniature version of a tow lift at a ski resort. It stood still, apparently unused for years, and if it had worked I could only imagine the jarring noise of ungreased wheels completely destroying the silence of the reading room. I avoided the tow lift, followed the librarian, turned right, walked a few more spaces, turned left, followed her around the corner and then right up a very short flight of stairs. I had entered a labyrinth and had forgotten to drop bread crumbs to find my way back.

At the top of the stairs, four little desks formed a small reading room of their own. The ceiling had not been raised, so the desks sat on what was essentially a half floor, like the half floors at Butler Library but with a much lower ceiling; my head was now about 1 meter closer to the ceiling. This was a tiny and very dusty space. On three sides, I was surrounded by more books on more sagging shelves. These volumes looked as if they had been unread for centuries. I could look down the stairs from where I had come or I could look a few yards ahead with a view to what appeared to be the outside world. A small window pane with bumps and ridges in the glass—a symbol of aging building materials—looked onto a snowy street scene that I guessed was the courtyard of the library. In the courtyard I was pleased to see a car, even if it lay covered in snow and looked abandoned. The sight of the car suggested an escape route through the window and onto a street in the outside world. At the same time, it was impossible to position the courtyard relative to a known geographical landmark. Where was I? In a library in St. Petersburg, to be sure, but otherwise I was completely lost. If a fire had broken out, I would have burned to a crisp with my notes and the old books—since I planned to read about fires this was not all that disconcerting. The librarian brought the reading materials to me and, in near isolation, I settled down to read about late nineteenth-century conflagrations.

Luckily, no two library experiences are the same. The Russian National Library was conceived as a public library, but the word "public" referred to an educated public of the nineteenth century. It is now open to everyone, but it is still largely focused on academic matters. At the San Francisco Public Library, a more modern structure that blends into the skyline of San Francisco, the word "public" refers to every last soul in the city, even if pickier residents might not step onto the premises. Instead of screening visitors for academic accreditation, the library is public in the broadest sense of the word—it is open to anyone even if they have no interest in the books on the shelves. In contrast to the quiet and controlled spaces inside the St. Petersburg library, the public library in San Francisco is a raucous meeting place, albeit with a significant collection of scholarly books. The library in San Francisco faces challenges rarely seen in academic libraries, but it is no less a physical space of study as it holds government, mayoral, and other important papers. Since the library caters to a wide audience, it has to convince taxpayers of its legitimacy. An emphasis on video rentals, free Internet usage, and career seminars indicate the breadth of possible experiences. These programs create a paradox, because the scholar can find himself sitting next to a job seeker. In other words, the historian can research social welfare policies in San Francisco in the 1930s while sitting right next to someone who has fallen through the social welfare net in the year 2015.

The first time I walked into the San Francisco Public Library the police were escorting someone in handcuffs out of the building. The bustle of two policemen pushing along this disheveled individual was disconcerting, especially since a group of schoolchildren were heading in the other direction. The contrast was stark, but it anticipated other experiences. A visit to the washroom is a healthy first step to a long reading session at a library. Little did I expect to find the atmosphere of a campground washroom. Grizzled men were brushing their teeth, combing their hair, and even dabbing shaving cream onto their cheeks. The majority of the men in the toilets had large bags or backpacks—each bag contained a lifetime's worth of possessions or all the possessions of one life. Obviously, the washroom had become a peaceful sanctuary for the street dwellers of San Francisco.

The other floors on the library, which were open and inviting, were packed with readers, but the campground feeling still floated in the air because many readers had large backpacks at their feet—the traveler with the toothbrush in a bedroll comes to mind. On these upper floors, everyone respected the quiet and enjoyed whatever reading materials lay before them.

The open spaces in the San Francisco Public Library reflect new attitudes about physical spaces. Architects have accommodated modern needs. They have lightened up the atmosphere and transformed the dusty library with the stern librarian into a welcome space. Adjacent coffee shops, lounge chairs, and video monitors warm the visitor and eliminate the sense of intimidation associated with libraries. For instance, above the columns that adorn the façade of the Butler Library the architects had etched the names of famous intellectuals in stone. A visitor reading the names of Homer, Herodotus, Aristotle, and Demosthenes might be frightened away, not having read the works of these Mediterranean authors. But even at Butler, library architects are making the academic library experience less daunting—the first thing you experience upon entering the library is a little coffee shop. An open-space philosophy and an emphasis on technology predominate in contemporary design that favors comfort and convenience over endless nooks and crannies to store books.

In this respect, the new Bibliothèque Nationale de France, built in 1996, represents a hybrid of old and new. Large open spaces characterize the design of the building, but the spaces are separated by portals—that is, the doors give little indication of what lies on the other side. The reader has to pass through silver doors and go down escalators to get to the actual books, all the while being filled with a growing sense of anticipation. A North American who grew up during the 1970s might have flashbacks to the opening of the television program *Get Smart*, where Agent Smart passes through a series of doors before finally arriving at a telephone booth at the end of a corridor.

A sense of anticipation as well as mild disorientation already begins outside the library. You cannot just walk up to the library, knock on the door, and enter the building. The approach to the library takes the visitor up and down and left and right. From the east, the undulating Simone de Beauvoir footbridge crosses the Seine River and provides access to the library complex with its four large towers in the shape of open books. From the west side of the Seine, stairs from street level have to be mounted before stepping on the library campus. Once on the grounds of the library, wooden planks lead you toward a ramp that descends to the entrance—the vertical seesaw is a little unsettling. After this first descent, a security checkpoint has to be cleared before another descent. Here the visitor realizes that she will not be taking an elevator up into one of the towers, where one might expect to find a grandiose view of Paris. Instead, a lengthy escalator in a vast empty hall drops one into the reading areas. Down, down, down and the hustle and bustle of metropolitan Paris slowly fades away.

Rather unexpectedly you arrive to find a view onto a grand garden on the other side of great panes of glass, sunken from street level but open to the air. The courtyard defined by the space between the four towers is full of trees (the forest is clearly visible on Google Maps). The garden offers a natural state, perhaps the natural state of Jean-Jacques Rousseau, so the trappings of the consumer city above don't distract the earnest researcher. If the library staff decided to caulk the glass, pour in water and add fish, you would comfortably feel as if you were under the sea, far from the problems of land-based civilizations.

If the entry into this grandiose palace of books was not completely disorienting, you can take your leave from the garden and head to the specialized reading rooms that are situated off the corridors. Here the environment is much more familiar—librarians are ready to assist you while the rest of the readers are distributed at desks around the room. You just have to find a table, order some materials, and then you can begin to read an infinitesimally tiny portion of the total collection of the library.

The Bibliothèque Nationale in Paris, which has been storing books for centuries, naturally comes to mind when we think of famous international libraries. We might also add the Butler Library at Columbia University or the Widener Library at Harvard University. These institutions dazzle us with their renown and, of course, size—the Bibliothèque Nationale claims about 30 million volumes, the Columbia University libraries have about 10 million volumes, and the Harvard system claims more than 16 million volumes. These numbers are impressive and these traditional depositories are essential to the historian's craft. They are not, however, the only form of collection, because libraries exist in all shapes and colors. Preteens organize libraries in their basements and some adults store so many unreturned books in their apartments that the apartment space is transformed into a veritable branch library of its own. Importantly, specialized libraries float under the radar and often go unnoticed. For example, we take it for granted that we can check out a music CD at the public library, but we would be hard pressed to name a library devoted to music. These specialized libraries, hidden around the world, draw researchers into another physical environment.

The music library at the Juilliard School in the heart of New York City draws visitors into the cultural center of Manhattan. Nestled among the Metropolitan Opera House, the Walter Reade Theater and the Film Society of Lincoln Center, and the home of the New York City ballet, the Juilliard music library physically reminds visitors of the interconnectedness of the arts, humanities, and urban design. Despite the cacophony stored on the library shelves, the visitor can expect a quiet atmosphere in the reading rooms. The music stored on tapes, plastics, discs, paper, and whatever other material has been conducive to coding sound over the ages only speaks when spoken to. Unlike the broad mandate of a national library, the Juilliard library, with its associated archive, collects anything to do with music. With written biographies of composers and scores accessible to those who can read musical notation, the collection adds sound to research.

Presenting the Juilliard library as off the beaten path reflects a bit of prejudice. The average historian who concerns himself with political and social matters can happily ignore the Juilliard library and stay on safe territory at the Bibliothèque Nationale. In contrast, the historian of music could spend all her time at the Juilliard library and feel less at home in a standard academic library. This is a reflection of the numerous subdisciplines that exist under the umbrella heading of "history."

Historians do not always work indoors at library desks. They can travel to Rome to perform archaeological work or travel by sailboat in Polynesia to understand ancient migration patterns. In more recent times, the field of oral history has drawn the historian away from the desk and presented fundamental new research challenges and opportunities. Oral historians had to overcome long-standing prejudices within the historical profession because historians were so accustomed to written sources that they questioned the reliability of interviews. Oddly enough, historians trusted the transcriber of a court case more than they did the actual voice of the individual whose words were being written.

These attitudes have not been totally overcome, but oral history has entered the mainstream. As a result, oral historians cannot wait in their offices until individuals come to them. Rather, they must seek out individuals to interview and travel to those locations. The interview can take place in a living room, a kitchen, a restaurant, or in the park on a warm day. Depending on the cultural surroundings, the historian will have to eat food and drink while doing the research (I can vividly remember having three shots of cognac out of politeness before starting one interview). The historian will also confront language issues, whether in a foreign tongue or idiomatic speech with which he is not familiar.

Oral histories can take place anywhere in the world, and the historian has to chase them down. These oral histories will expose an individual familiar with libraries and seminar rooms to unexpected environments. If the historian wants to interview workers who had been involved in a protest a generation ago, she has to carefully consider how to approach the topic. Here the question "What should I wear?" has academic significance and can influence the gathering of information. Oral historians have clearly emphasized that they are not searching for absolute truths, so they fully understand how dress and attitude, for better and for worse, affect research. Furthermore, with the advancement of audio and video technologies, oral historians have tools that are vastly more complex than the traditional pen and paper. They can pack their iPad in their carry-on luggage and fly to a *favela* (an urban slum) in Rio de Janeiro. This image should also bring to the fore the gap between the social world of the historian and the social world of the individuals he studies.

Wandering around the country and the globe in search of historical traces has always been an exciting aspect of the profession and began with Herodotus. In the modern world flight makes travel easier, but historians also have to deal with unexpected circumstances. During the Cold War, the communist powers in the Eastern Bloc kept track of historians who visited the region. A historian might be summoned to the offices of the US Central Intelligence Agency to be warned that he would be followed when he arrived in Moscow. The historian should not be worried but, at the same time, should not try to evade the Soviet agent. The secret services in these countries also hired informants and kept files on what the historian was doing. Over the years, the informants wrote reports that could add up to thousands of pages. Unbeknownst to researchers, the secret service could subtly steer Western research agendas. Instead of just passively reporting on the activities of the historian, the government would ensure that the Western researcher came into contact with a renowned local scholar. This renowned scholar, who understood his marching orders, would recommend books to read and sources to pursue. He directed the unsuspecting historian to conversations with specific individuals while intentionally steering her away from others. All of this adds to the complexity of the research process. More basically, however, it situates the historian as a curious human being who finds herself in an endless range of unexpected situations.

This discussion has targeted those physical spaces that historians frequent to add a third dimension to two-dimensional texts. It cannot be exhaustive since each individual historian writes up his own itinerary and follows it however he pleases. But even if we leave the comprehensive travel log for another day, we won't lose sense of the mobile aspect of historical research. To uncover meaningful documents, the historian cannot afford to wait for them to come to her or until they have been neatly digitized and packaged online. The above examples might even suggest that the bookish historian needs a sense of intrepidity and adventure. Moreover, the physical spaces and linguistic environment will actually impact research. Many scholars shy away from Russian history because the thought of visiting such a cold country has little appeal; in contrast, studying the Italian Renaissance brings more comfortable rewards. Similarly, the physical environment of the archives and libraries mentioned in this narrative have a gravitational force to pull historians out of their offices. In effect, the homebody will have a harder time exploring the past.

Chapter 2

THE SOURCES WE USE

Whenever the historian moves from place to place, he is always in search of new sources. In whatever form they arrive, the sources will be foundational to the analysis. In the archives the historian can read archival documents, and in the library she can sift through old books. In the nineteenth century, when the historical profession was just getting started, these were certainly the two most popular sources. Nowadays, the source base has become much more diversified, reflecting the complexity of the modern world. The fictional novel was formerly approached with a cynical eye but now enjoys respect in historical works. Similarly, older generations of historians were deeply suspicious about oral testimony because they considered it little more than chatter that was overburdened by the subjectivity of the speaker—anything of importance would most certainly have been written down. Today, innovative projects like StoryCorps are recording thousands of oral histories and depositing the recordings in sanctuaries like the Library of Congress in Washington, DC. With the acceptance of the nontextual, visual sources have also garnered greater attention. Film and photography are no longer mere illustrations of textual points but are significant in their own right. Despite the growing diversity, potential sources still get overlooked.

This chapter takes a closer look at the materials a historian could expect to find and use. In each case, the historian has to approach the materials with a careful eye. As E.H. Carr once wrote, it is the duty and not a praiseworthy accomplishment of the historian to get the facts right. Yet with the diversity of sources there is no single way to interpret the information drawn from these sources. Without delving deeply into philosophical questions concerning the nature of facts, we can still highlight the distinct challenges these sources present and reveal the process through which the historian analyzes them. This discussion exposes the multilayered environment of the primary sources historians listen to, read, watch, touch, and smell.

By the middle of the twentieth century, archives had become the standard for historical research, especially since they had been popularized from the nineteenth century onwards. They have lost their dominant position today but, as evident from the last chapter, they still command respect from historians. So what can one expect from the materials? What does a historian hope to accomplish?

I once joked to a friend that I had been in the reading room when a centenarian stood up, cheered, and proudly proclaimed he had read every document in the archive. This would, of course, be impossible since archives are vast. The section of the Ministry of Internal Affairs of the Russian Empire has at least 500,000 files, each file possibly containing hundreds of pages. The historian will only ever read a tiny portion of the available files, whatever subject he decides to focus on. Despite the depressing knowledge that you will never make a dent in all those materials, how can the historian work through them?

Normally, there are two ways to organize files. In the first case the archive simply adopts the materials in the way they were originally ordered. The materials can be catalogued in the same divisions as the actual ministry, and the individual files packaged much as they would have been by the bureaucrat; in a sense, the historian ends up leafing through the desk of different bureaucrats. In the second case, the archivists can sift through the original materials and sort them according to a common theme. This was a popular method in the Soviet Union, where archivists brought together all the revolutionary material they could find. Archivists could then remove sensitive or counterrevolutionary pages. For example, the Archive of Contemporary History in Moscow has a Chernobyl section, but the files have been carefully curated for the researcher (leaving the researcher asking for more).

When the archival file lands on your desk, you begin sifting through 2 to 200 pages or even 2,000 pages. Every file is met with trepidation (How can I possibly read all this stuff? Will I find the missing link?), but one very quickly finds the trends in documents. Since many files maintain the original ordering, the historian can see who was communicating with whom, what issues continued to pop up, and who had responsibility for them. If you open a file from the Ministry of Internal Affairs devoted to spring floods, you can already make some conclusions. The very existence of the file suggests the state was not indifferent to seasonal catastrophes. Since the state produced the documents it will be difficult to judge whether it dealt with the problem sufficiently, but you have a starting point for judgment. If the file contains correspondence with the Ministry of Agriculture, you have grounds for thinking that the state had an economic rather than environmental or health interest when the snow started to melt. Of course, these would only be preliminary posits that would require further substantiation.

Although the documents have an order to them, reading archival material is not quite like reading a neatly bound book. The files do not contain uniform cuts of paper. Scraps of all sizes, from telegrams to personal letters to imperial letterhead, surface between the covers of the files. By piecing together these scraps, the historian can create a web of interactions from the past. Often the historian will be reading through handwritten correspondences from the nineteenth century. The handwriting of trained scribes is easier to decipher than the scrawl of Friedrich Nietzsche or the alchemist notation of Newton, but the handwriting presents certain challenges, especially when penned in a script other than our own. The situation became easier with the invention of the typewriter and easier still with computer documents (though here the sheer volume of data creates entirely new problems). When you return the documents, your own little bit of history is left behind, because your fingerprints now lie invisibly on these older pieces of paper.

If archival documents are published, historians can access documents by checking a book out of the library and reading the papers in the comfort of their living room. This eliminates the excitement of traveling to an archive, but more importantly the historian cannot be quite sure what she is getting. A half century ago, E.H. Carr wrote about the strange publication history of the papers of Gustav Stresemann, a German statesman of the Weimar period (roughly during the 1920s). Stresemann left behind boxes of personal papers that he had already sifted through to anchor his reputation for posterity. The German publishers then culled through these papers to issue a highly selective book on Stresemann's activities. Since German diplomacy was of interest in England, a British publisher translated the German work but did a selective translation, leaving out what the editors believed would be of little interest to English-speaking readers. According to Carr, this process wiped out German activities on the eastern front during World War I from the historical record. Nevertheless, these edited volumes were considered objective because they reflected the earnest decisions of an earnest state (though the processing skewed interpretation). The historian was mistakenly encouraged not to worry about the papers' validity because they had already been processed.

The archive has, however, been forced to yield much of its influence as the profession expanded in unexpected directions. One major shift was the willingness of historians to employ novels as primary sources. For generations, historians had downplayed fiction because it reeked of uncertainty—and uncertainty made historians uncomfortable. Today, however, fiction has a vital role in historical writing and has shifted the subject of analysis. As military and political histories waned in popularity, historians looked to novelists to help answer a new set of questions about social and cultural habits. A willingness to read novels required more time in a library than an archive.

As a source, a novel can have several functions. In mid-nineteenth-century France, the realist novels of Gustave Flaubert gave close insights into the lives of fictional characters designed after living prototypes. *Madame Bovary* exposed readers to the mundane aspects of adultery in provincial society. In this respect, the novel informs historians about societal values, a growing new readership and, when corroborated with other sources, social habits in the provinces. At about the same time in Russia, Fyodor Dostoyevsky was also weaving fact and fiction into his novels. While *Demons* was and is a fictional novel, it embodied the tensions surrounding the Russian nihilist movement in the middle of the nineteenth century. Strictly speaking, the characters did not personify the values of a single nihilist, even though characters were modeled after living people and certain events in the novel were based on the violent actions of nihilists. Rather, the fictional characters carefully reflected the dominant values of those radical circles. Dostoyevsky, a contemporary to these events, portrayed the shortcomings of these radical youth in his attempt to promote an Orthodox alternative. The novel therefore not only represents Dostoyevsky's analysis of a nonfictional situation, but also his antidote. In an ideal situation, his nonfiction readers would be swayed by his persuasive writing and thus he could influence the political views of his readers. The novel responded to an existing nonfictional historical situation to shape a future nonfictional situation.

Other novels are useful because they remind historians of issues that might otherwise be overlooked. In this sense, they don't provide data but they point to potential sources of data. George Gissing's *The Odd Women* revealed the fate of women in late Victorian England who did not marry. These single women were pushed to the periphery of society and led lives worthy of historical attention; the novel encourages research into single Victorian women in alternate sources. Moreover, the book explains a sensitive historical situation to students who might otherwise never come across a similar issue. The novel cannot reveal the decisions of statesmen or statistical details about the economic plight of single urban women, but it nevertheless opens up further avenues of research. The significance of the novel to historians had to wait until the historical profession became more sensitive to the role of women in history.

Although a complicated topic, *The Odd Women* points to a social issue in a straightforward way. Other novels require more intricate analysis to relate them to issues of historical interest. Detective novels, pulp fiction, erotica, and science-fiction novels do not clearly set an agenda for the historian; a little more curiosity is required to highlight their worth to historical analysis. Philip Marlowe, Raymond Chandler's famous private investigator, did not answer historical questions about Los Angeles. But the mood created in the book provides the reader with a darker vision of Los Angeles than one typically finds on postcards of the beach.

Even if these novels were never intended to become part of the historical record, they nonetheless have a place in historical analysis. In part, the current interest of historians determines this place. When military history dominated scholarship, historians ignored the erotic novel unless they read this prose for pleasure in their spare time; even then they did not dare footnote this source in a serious historical work. As the nature of historical questioning changed, though, so too did the value of the source. Today an erotic novel can answer any number of respectable questions. The Victorian era was notorious for its prudish attitude and unwillingness to talk about sex. Thus the very existence of eroticism in a novel from the nineteenth century, such as George W.M. Reynolds's *The Mysteries of London*, suggests the

Victorians did have sexual desires that were fulfilled. When historians discovered evidence that women also read erotic novels, they gained clues about the social and sexual behavior of this group. Historians can investigate how sexual themes shifted over time to gain an understanding of what a man expected from an erotic novel and how authors developed new techniques to objectify the sexuality of women. Likewise we can read Proust to open up questions about homosexuality in old age. The changing contours of the erotic novel can help explain shifting moral codes, publishing laws, and the habits of specific economic classes. These conclusions will depend on the portrayal of the protagonists and the situations in which the authors placed them. They also force the historian to look for sources lying outside the novel. We cannot just blindly trust Proust's depiction of homosexual Paris during World War I, but surely he was onto something.

An interesting variation on this theme, one developed during the 1970s, is to read nonfictional historical documents with a literary eye. Historians who wanted to challenge the objective qualities of factual evidence argued that even nonfiction documents were constructed with literary devices. These theorists argued that the nineteenth-century historian did not pen an objective historical account, but instead an account with a preconceived plot, a rising tension between protagonists and antagonists, a climax in which the tensions were resolved, and a denouement to release the reader from the tensions. This method has its limits since it is difficult to show how mundane bureaucratic documents or party statements fit a literary mold, but it is a further reminder of how literary techniques can be incorporated into historical analysis.

If novels were left at the margins for decades, visual sources suffered a worse fate. Novels, despite the fictional content, had the advantage of being written in a mode of presentation that was familiar to historians who worked with texts. Visual sources, in contrast, were foreign and too popular to be taken seriously. Art historians had their artists, but should the historian pay attention to an *Illustrated Weekly* from the late nineteenth century and risk overlooking important diplomatic sources? Whether in film or photography, serious visual scholarship had to confront the reality that leading scholarly journals rarely, if ever, published images. When images were published, they arrived as handmaidens to the textual evidence. This prejudice was the outcome of a time when historians studied intellectual and political history. Fortunately, visual sources have become increasingly important and might even dominate analysis in the decades ahead. Here we can look at the role of film and photography as visual sources.

Around the world, there are millions upon millions of feet of film negative. In this context, we can distinguish between three different types of films. First there are narrative films with a historical subject, like *Gone with the Wind*. Second there are narrative films with no real pretensions to address a historical subject, such as *Star Wars*, that offer insights into the values of the time when the film was made. Third there are the infinite amounts of scraps of film, such as home videos, newsreels, and random footage, that are lying in archives, basements, and garages around the world. Each of these variants has a different value for the historian.

In early silent films, such as D.W. Griffith's *The Birth of a Nation* (1915) or Sergei Eisenstein's *Battleship Potemkin* (1925), the viewer is presented with key historical episodes—the Civil War in the American case and the revolution of 1905 in the Russian case. Visually, each film carefully dramatizes specific historical epochs, and their dramatic power lures viewers into accepting the historical presentation at face value. Even when contemporaries recognized the factual limitations of the films, they filled a need. *The Birth of a Nation* was criticized for its historical inaccuracies but, as film historians have noted, Americans preferred to hear and see these inaccuracies.

Today, *The Birth of a Nation* strikes the viewer as odd and even laughable because of scenes that portray the Ku Klux Klan as heroes who save the fate of an American town. The film, however, clearly indicated the structure of persisting racist values 50 years after the US Civil War. As a source, therefore, the visual imagery of the film is less important than the social furor it caused upon its release. The film became a recruiting piece for the Ku Klux Klan and mobilized the National Association for the Advancement of Colored People to protest the most blatant racist scenes. Therefore, even if the film says absolutely nothing about the Civil War in the middle of the nineteenth century, the public response offers the historian a toehold into the values of Americans at the start of the twentieth century.

Sergei Eisenstein's *Battleship Potemkin* is as important as Griffith's masterpiece in the history of film because it plays a similar role when historians contemplate the history of the Russian Revolution. In 1905 Russia experienced its first revolution, and throughout the empire protests broke out for economic, social, and ethnic reasons. Twenty years after the event the Soviet state commissioned Eisenstein to create a film version of the events that took place throughout the Russian Empire. In the minds of Soviet authorities, film had distinct advantages when the majority of citizens still could not read. Eisenstein began the project in St. Petersburg, but bad weather forced him south and he visited Baku on the Caspian Sea before settling on Odessa, a famous Black Sea port city, as the film's location. Once in Odessa, however, the broad plans of the film were dropped and Eisenstein depicted 1905 through a single event in a single city. In 1905, sailors on the Battleship Potemkin refused to eat maggot-infested meat and a mutiny on the ship ensued; the sailors gained the sympathy of Odessans and a battle erupted between the tsarist forces and the residents of the city. In contrast to Griffiths, Eisenstein paid careful attention to historical events and interviewed residents who had experienced the 1905 events in Odessa. It is therefore tempting to claim that *Battleship Potemkin* is more historically accurate than *The Birth of a Nation* (even if it only depicts events in Odessa).

Although historical films are often evaluated in terms of accuracy, this is a misleading standard. Studios make painstaking efforts to ensure that the costumes, styles, and street scenes in movies match the historical period in question; the viewer is then lured into believing that the historical value of the film is reflected in the studio's successful matching of a starlet's dress to the era that slides across the silver screen. Film understood in this manner has only limited appeal for the historian because it says more about the research of the directors and their staff than it does about interpreting the past.

Instead, film can be employed and analyzed in other, more creative perspectives. Scholars of film history can focus on developing techniques of montage and theoretical influences on directors. For example, the revolutionary influences on Eisenstein were inspired by the dialectic method of classic Marxism and leave strong visual traces in his films. Montage sequences are intended to contrast and form a dialectic—thesis/antithesis—to push the interpretation to the next level. When studying these philosophical parameters, film historians pay less attention to its historical contents.

Alternatively, the film can be watched to analyze Soviet values almost a decade after the revolution of 1917. *Battleship Potemkin* offers clues about the Soviets' interpretation of their own revolutionary history. Approached from this perspective, the historical component of the film is less compelling than the historical circumstances in which the film was made. It is not 1905 but 1925, the year the film was produced, that becomes the topic of research.

Eisenstein and his crew certainly researched the events of 1905, but their vision of 1905 was conditioned by the revolution of 1917—without the revolution of 1917, 1905 would have been portrayed in a different manner. Produced only eight years after the revolution, the young Soviet state had only just started to evaluate the meaning of the revolution; revolutionary artists competed to create a vision of what the revolution had been and what the Soviet state would become. Thus *Battleship Potemkin* evinces the mood of the 1920s, when filmmakers, authors, and architects experimented with the past. In later years, Soviet authorities rethought the meaning of the revolution and cinematic themes shifted. Whereas *Battleship Potemkin* (1925) did not contain elements of Russian nationalism, *Alexander Nevsky* (1938), a film about the thirteenth-century prince who mobilized Russians to defeat an invasion by the Teutonic Knights, clearly did. The shift from a strictly class-based presentation of events to a film with nationalist tendencies indicates how Soviet society had changed from 1925 to 1938. Thus the historical accuracy about Nevsky in the thirteenth century or Odessa at the start of the twentieth century has marginal weight when looking at the value of the source.

Historians can also study entertainment in popular films to understand shifts in societal and political moods. *The Graduate* (1967) has cultural significance because it challenged suburban mores in America. The *Rocky* films may have little aesthetic or directorial appeal, but they remind historians how Americans reacted to the Cold War and the threat of communism. The television series *Happy Days* suggests to the historian how viewers during the 1970s wanted to envision gender roles and social structures from the 1950s (note how the interaction of time periods complicates the research of the historian). Howard Cunningham played the role of a steady father and self-employed individual, thus his role might suggest nostalgia for a bygone era—although determining whether that bygone era ever existed would require sources external to the sitcom.

Historians do not have to satisfy themselves with American films. Soviet films of the 1960s and 1970s evince shifts in the importance of communist ideology and the growth of Western influence beyond the Iron Curtain. In

White Sun of the Desert (1970), viewers are exposed to what has been called a Spaghetti Eastern. The directors drew freely from American films but set *White Sun of the Desert* on the territory of the Soviet Union. In *To the Black Sea* (1957), a romantic film about a road trip two students took, historians are exposed to the importance of car culture in the Soviet mind as well as the possibilities women had to drive cars. In *The Irony of Fate* (1975), viewers are offered a comedic look at the effects of excessive alcohol consumption and a critique of modern Soviet apartment blocks. These films don't merely state facts about the existence of cars or the woes of apartment living, they also suggest the regime's ability to laugh at itself as well as the limits of acceptable criticism. Moreover, the continual presence of standard consumer goods can suggest to the historian that, despite the communist veneer, basic Soviet values were not that dissimilar from their American counterparts.

In the past 10 years many American and foreign films have become readily available on YouTube in a way that archival documents have not. We might be tempted to criticize a historian who published a book five years ago and neglected these films as sources. Five years ago, however, these films were unavailable and beyond the purview of the historian. On the one hand, forgiveness is in order; on the other hand, next time round these sources cannot afford to be overlooked.

All the films mentioned so far involve studios, actors, budgets, and institutions, and this also explains why they are now so readily available on YouTube. But not all video footage emerges from an institutional setting. Despite the progress of digitizing sources, archives have yet to place substantial random footage on the web, though massive collections of interesting footage exist. In 1990, two German film directors released *Mein Krieg* (*My Private War*), which featured films made by Nazi soldiers on the eastern front. These soldiers were film buffs, not official photographers. They had small 8-mm cameras in their pockets and shot film randomly in their spare moments. Instead of dramatic war footage, the viewer sees relaxed German soldiers taking a break, Russian peasants at work, or even a young Russian woman doing a striptease for the invading soldiers. The images are dramatically different than the standard war footage and humanize the experience of these German soldiers, even if this is not a feeling we desire.

Similarly, archives devoted specially to films hold endless random fragments from the past. When historians order materials from these establishments, they don't receive a stack of papers bound in a file folder. More likely than not they receive a stack of dented canisters and have to run the film through the reels of the viewing apparatus by themselves. If they can get that far, then a virtually untapped resource unfolds—it is difficult to predict what one might find since the resources are so immense. A scholar interested in natural disasters can find snippets of eyewitness footage and, more importantly, see how first responders interacted with the victims. A scholar of sports can find footage from matches to understand the social divisions among sporting fans or slowly trace the transition from public stadiums to corporate stadiums. Reels can also display aspects of working-class or domestic life that have gone unnoticed. It might be impossible to discover who was responsible for taking the footage, but the variety of perspectives is crucial.

Photography has a longer history than film but has also created challenges and presented the historian with similar dilemmas. The invention of photography in the nineteenth century created an opportunity to document the world in a seemingly realistic, objective, and scientific fashion. Exposure times and cumbersome equipment placed limits on its effectiveness, but intrepid photographers embarked on world tours to record events. In the 1850s, Roger Fenton traveled to the Crimean Peninsula and photographed the famous Valley of the Shadow of Death. Visual evidence gained in significance as the photograph was considered more epistemologically reliable than a painting or printed lithograph (and also became part of crime investigations). Over the past 150 years, photographic techniques have improved considerably; the world is more photographed than ever and future generations of historians will have easy access to billions of photographs.

Despite the abundance of visual representations, the photograph has often been underappreciated as a source, both in its usefulness and in its complexity. Outside the field of art history, historians have traditionally treated photographs as illustrations to accompany text. In this form, the photograph facilitates an understanding of the historian's writing but it is not evidence itself. For example, Peter Hall's *Cities in Civilization* has photographs presented in clusters throughout the book. The photograph of Florence and the street scene of Paris with the *fiacres* and the *flâneurs* visualize textual arguments. A.J.P. Taylor's illustrated history of World War I employs photographs to bring the deadly struggle to life. But the photographs are not subject to analysis in the same way that the discussions of diplomats are. The photograph is made subservient to the textual analysis.

When photographs are presented as illustrations, the viewer is lured into believing that they are observing a frozen moment from the past—the street scene is just that, a street scene. This false sense of objectivity has its parallel in scholarly writing that refrains from using the first person to give the narrative a sense of detachment. By removing the author from the past, this style suggests we have unmediated access to that past. Unwittingly, the reader forgets that a historian stands between the past and the text. Likewise, when photos are presented as mere illustrations we overlook the photographer who stood between the street scene and our view of it.

Once we take the position of the photographer into consideration, the photograph as a source becomes much more complex. Felice Beato, an Italian photojournalist from the nineteenth century, traveled to India where he photographed the Indian Rebellion (also referred to as the Sepoy Mutiny) of 1857. In one image, the viewer sees a scaffold with hanged rebels. Importantly, the photograph does not just memorialize death; it has to be considered in its broadest possible context—the viewer must consider that Beato, his European values, and his equipment belong to the larger scene. While the hanged men stopped paying attention, all the sentient beings in the image were aware of Beato and his equipment. The presence of a European affected the behavior and mannerisms of individuals at the site. As a source, then, the photograph certainly tells the story of a hanging but it also indicates the multifaceted ways in which European imperialism, through the export of its recent industrial and technological advances, influenced local society. When placed in the history of war photography, Beato's image will tell yet another story.

Since photographic images are so compelling to the eye, the contexts of those producing the imagery have to be qualified. Was the photographer on commission from someone at home? Was it a newspaper with a political leaning or royals with their own concerns? These questions suggest that the photographer can develop a selective visual history, in the process ignoring other moments in time. At the turn of the last century, the photographer Jacob Riis took a radical step when he decided to photograph the slums in New York City, thus focusing on the neglected and forgotten. His photographs belong to a specific worldview and political inclination.

Riis's work with flash photography, a recent invention, indicates how technologies foreign to historians often determine the nature of sources. The absence of technologies limited how and when a photograph could be taken. Without the ability to lighten dark spaces, photographers had restrictions on where they could take pictures. When new technologies dramatically improved street lighting toward the end of the nineteenth century, photographers had an expanded field for practicing their craft. Technologies also skewed situations—it is well known that flash photography adds light where there is none. In societies fascinated with artificial lighting, the addition of external light can suggest a more optimistic view (even when looking at dire images) than the circumstances warrant. Images can also overdetermine interpretation if the researcher is not careful. If we only have photographs of the downtown core of Paris in the nineteenth century, we can be tempted to conclude that everyone lived in prosperity. Impressions will change when faced with a batch of photographs from another part of town.

Furthermore, photographs present the viewer with temporal dilemmas. The Parisian street scene mentioned above suggests a frozen moment in time and space; instinctively, we accept that the image came about during a measurable time interval. Despite the apparent temporal certainty, the meaning of the photograph changes over a long time duration. We can pinpoint the moment when the photographer opened the lens, but that moment is but the beginning of a developing story. As people and societies undergo transformations, photographs are read in varied ways. A bourgeois street scene from late nineteenth-century Paris can be interpreted as the successful rise of industrial society or as the dominant symbol of a strict and repressive moral code. The wedding photo of a couple who got divorced after 10 years of marriage has no fixed meaning. The still photograph, probably no different from millions of other wedding photographs, radically changes as the relationship deteriorates. Whereas the young newlyweds looked upon the photograph with happiness and hope, the divorced wife glances at the same image with regret and remorse. The physical photograph has not changed at all, but its meaning—its most important element—has been transformed radically.

Additional examples come to mind. A photograph of a German soldier taken in 1915 is interpreted differently when viewed in 1925 or 1955 or 1995. In 1925, it served as a reminder of a horrific war, one not to be repeated. In

1955, the experiences of Nazi Germany would be superimposed on earlier memories, for it is impossible to eliminate the negative aspects of the Nazi period when interpreting the photograph. By 1995, a degree of reconciliation will have been made with the Nazi past and the viewer will hesitate to condemn the image as would have been the case in 1955. The viewer can see both a human being with moral values and a symbol of Nazi wickedness even if the uniform predates the Nazis. And in 2095, the photograph will embody another set of values altogether.

Television as a visual source has numerous possibilities for future research. Formerly, television was frowned upon by academics; scholars were supposed to read about life, not let it pass as a couch potato. Scholars who did watch television never dreamed of footnoting TV programs that were meant to be entertainment and not subjects of analysis. Over the years, however, television has developed a dominant presence and it will be hard to look back on the late twentieth century without considering the global impact of television. In the early 1980s, Gary Larson poked fun at this in a *Far Side* cartoon entitled "In the Days before Television." A family was shown staring at an empty wall. The cartoon commented on how the placement of a television shaped the spaces in which we live. Today, public spaces such as airports, bars, and restaurants are largely defined by the placement of televisions. The recent transition to flat-screen televisions has made this device more omnipresent than ever.

Beyond the physical presence of televisions, the ever-changing content available on television has to be considered in any history of American politics and society (since many politicians spend lots of time watching television as well). On average, Americans watch over 20 hours of television a week. In the past, historians would pay scant attention to this statistic and simply lament on the lost time. It has become increasingly apparent that even if an individual watches only 20 hours a week, almost all their major decisions are based on the exposure they had to television. Votes cast in elections depend on televised campaign ads and the contents of news shows; economic choices stem from luring advertisements as well as information provided in market analyses. Attitudes to social issues such as gay marriage and immigrant rights are mediated through sitcoms, talk shows, and other formats. Even the decision to pay for cable TV and access these channels enters into the equation.

Soon historians will not be able to avoid television even if they have no specific interest in television per se. They will need viewing statistics to understand which demographic groups watched the shows and how changes in programming reflect social attitudes, and to search for links between these shows and the outcomes of political events. Historians will need to be able to access old news programs and other items of importance. At an international level, historians will have to watch Italian and Chinese television shows to make similar historical claims about those societies. Since many historians are trained to read languages and not necessarily listen to them, this will add a level of difficulty to the training of the historian. Nevertheless, we will just have to accept a symbiotic relationship between the "power on" button of the television and life itself.

All these visual sources are filled with unfamiliar objects worthy of their own study. The same Parisian street scene has thousands of discrete objects scattered about; despite their appearance they get pushed to the side of the frame. These objects provide further traces of the past, but their usefulness depends on whether the historian wishes to use them statically or dynamically. Traditionally, objects have been associated with static displays in museums. In natural history museums of the late nineteenth century, curators presented preserved insects and curiosities from the natural world. We look at these objects without considering the shifting environments in which they existed. In his work on Greek homosexuality, K.J. Dover examined the erotic images on vases to investigate the nature of male love in antiquity. The emphasis was placed on the images on the object and not the object's role in different situations. For example, how did the images on the vases affect discussion as the vases were passed from hand to hand? This is a difficult question to answer given an absence of reliable sources, but in other instances the same question highlights the importance of understanding sources dynamically.

Nowadays, objects are considered in a dynamic rather than static manner, suggesting clues to the dynamism of living environments. For example, the Wende Museum in Los Angeles collects furniture and household goods from communist East Germany to preserve aspects of that civilization (and do more than collect endless speeches and directives of party leaders). When historians study these objects, they situate them relative to specific issues— the role of consumer culture, fashion influences from the West, the social strata that purchased such goods, how the goods influenced social inter-action, and so on. In fact, objects have become such a source of inspiration that they have become the butt of an important joke. In 1979, David Macaulay published *Motel of the Mysteries*, a story set in the very distant future. The protagonist of the story, an archaeologist named Howard Carson, stumbles upon an ancient American motel and draws erroneous conclusions about American civilization based on the objects he finds. The archaeologist can-not resist the temptation to overanalyze the most banal and commonplace situations. One cartoon depicts a messy hotel room with a television, remote control, and all the other trappings of late twentieth-century American soci-ety; the story disparagingly describes the archaeologist's analysis of the bed-room scene and misinterpretation of everyday objects. The story mocks a scholarly trend to overanalyze, but thinking about objects permits the his-torian to move away from straightforward textual analysis. It is an excellent pedagogical exercise to present students of any age with an object and ask them to consider how the object "led its life."

What can a remote control in the hotel room or a telephone from the 1940s tell us? What argument can a historian build from these sources? If a historian finds a telephone from the 1940s at a flea market, she can argue that the technology for telephones was available in the 1940s, but the value of the object as a source is not always related to the technological or practi-cal function of the object. Objects belong in physical places and determine social dynamics much like the layout of the family home affects how people meet. Curious minds can determine the situations in which the object found itself and how the object intersected and even altered the lives of humans—a phone suggests connections to the outside world, though we might not yet know what those connections were. Similarly, a statue in a park frames the worldview of passersby who are reminded of a local hero or an ancient strug-gle; an old tire can be symbolic of decaying industrial cities or a youth swing-ing under trees in a suburban home. When the historian understands these multiple lives, he gains a greater toehold on the past. Of course, the historian needs to visit locales that have these objects and consider some very practical aspects of them: How heavy are they? Do they smell? How do they wear?

Objects are not always single things with easily identifiable contours. His-torians have adopted a method (what might be called spice-rack history) to explore how objects, such as spices, have different meanings depending on where they appear in the world. Inspired by Sidney Mintz's anthropological study of sugar, historians have traced the social, economic, and political paths of global items that became dominant in European imperial trade patterns. Books on nutmeg, cinnamon, and whatever other spice you can imagine follow the object from its cultivation in or around the Spice Islands to the plate in European homes. Along the way, historians studied plantation conditions, slave labor, the packaging and advertising of said spice, and the evolution of European culinary traditions that were, in fact, deeply influenced by Asian and Indian produce. By focusing on a simple object such as a little seed of nutmeg, historians could show interconnections between all the globe's continents well before the advent of the global village.

These spice studies introduced a spatial dimension that has often been forgotten when considering the past. Textual analysis all too often loses the spatial component when historical actors are referenced with names or countries are treated as individuals ("Germany wanted to . . ."). The names act as little more than labels, and the complex physical environment in which the objects of analysis lived is ignored. The employment of objects balances the analysis and inserts an important dimension.

In this spirit, an additional dimension has left invisible traces in the past as well. Absent in most texts, sound has played a fundamental role in human history. Consider the following paradox: A historian sitting in a quiet library with a librarian at hand to shush excessive noises might still be reading an incredibly loud text. Even if a pin could be heard if dropped in the reading room, the book can describe armor clashing, women screaming, glass breaking, and bells ringing. An aural canyon exists between the atmosphere in which the historian is reading the text and the sounds that have been reduced to adjectives in the text.

The meaning of sound as an integral source requires exploration. Sound has far too often been overlooked and faces even greater challenges than visual sources. A few thinkers made sound integral to their thought—Arthur Schopenhauer and Friedrich Nietzsche philosophized about music—but these were isolated cases. Moreover, noise and sound involve more than just music.

To appreciate how the ear can be transformed into a source for historians, the next few pages examine how the sound waves that strike individual ears can be worthy of attention. The aural component of historical analysis can be divided into three categories: music, noise, and sound. The first category requires no direct explanation, whereas noise and sound do. Noises are considered random—such as a working sawmill, a train's whistle—and only accidentally affect our hearing. Noise can be birds chirping, trees creaking, footsteps on cobblestones, or the wind rustling through whatever it chooses. In other words, no authority has consciously determined that we must listen to them. Sounds, on the other hand, require more strategic planning from those who produce them. Church bells, music piped into shopping malls, a radio in the kitchen, and the scores played at sporting events are specifically designed to affect our behavior.

Music is probably the most straightforward of the three categories because it has already garnered the attention of many experts. Historians have long since examined the relationship between folk customs and classical music. At the start of the twentieth century, Béla Bartók collected songs from his native Hungary and incorporated this music in his formal compositions. The links between music and political functions are hardly unknown. Historians of music carefully situate composers into a political framework. Georg Friedrich Handel, for example, arrived in England in 1710 and entered an unsettled society still reeling from the revolutions of the seventeenth century. At a time when patronage of music and attendance at the opera house were linked to political interests, Handel's music had political ramifications. Thus historians have studied his political leanings and his ability to navigate between competing sides. It is no surprise to learn that his music was an important component of the royal image. In 1722, Handel's music was played at the Chapel Royal when King George I returned safely to London after the Atterbury plot (a plot to overthrow the king) had been discovered. When George I died in 1727, Handel composed coronation anthems for the next king, George II. In the future, historians will no doubt examine the role of Beyoncé at the inauguration of President Barack Obama in 2013.

As a primary source, music belongs in a social and political context: Who performed it? Who was the intended audience and what message was the music meant to convey? Beyond the social context, musicologists explore creative tonalities and experimental aspects in music. This analysis becomes wedded to intricate musical techniques that require specialist knowledge even within the historical profession. When historical musicologists pay less attention to the king's political needs, their attitude reflects that of the film historian who is more concerned with the history of film techniques than the political impact of the film. The intricacies of the musical composition will most likely remain foreign to general historians, though this does not prevent the general historian from analyzing a musical work's social and political impact.

This phenomenon has parallels with a general historian of science who is probably unable to explain the mechanics of a steam locomotive but understands the social importance of the locomotive. By the middle of the nineteenth century locomotives produced noise that changed aural experiences in the countryside. A farmer accustomed to the cock-a-doodle-do of the rooster now had to deal with the horn of the iron rooster. The puffs of steam and the clang of steel, signs of industrialization and urbanization, now penetrated the countryside. The noise of the locomotive was accidental or a byproduct of engine design, but it was not insignificant.

Over the ages, a variety of incidental noises have played a critical role in history. Beyond the barnyard noises, we tend to think of rural villages as bastions of tranquility in a world slowly overwhelmed by industrial noise. But what about the villagers who lived near the sawmill? How did the villagers get a good night's sleep when the mill created a racket as it made planks from freshly cut timber? Since so much behavior is conditioned by the amount of sleep we get, how did such a noise affect social behavior or even enter into the dreams of the villagers? Other noises could inadvertently trigger a host of thoughts. The hooves of a horse could signal the arrival of a nobleman, the police seeking to arrest someone, or army officials on a mission to conscript young men. These random and spontaneous noises established a familiar profile for inhabitants—when the noises changed, so did the expectations of the inhabitants.

These noises have been around for centuries, but they are elusive in written sources. In most written documents the soundtrack is missing. The majority of speeches give few clues about the voice of the speaker, the amplification of the voice, or the aural response to the text. Historians have to extract the noise from silent sources and then consider how the noise will form part of the investigation. Even when the tones of speeches were recorded the historian has to tread carefully. In the transcriptions of speeches presented at meetings of the Bolshevik party in 1917 and beyond, the transcribers often inserted comments such as "[applause]" to give more vocal support to the leadership. The insertion was part of a broader political strategy to promote a specific view, so the historian has no guarantee that the noise actually occurred. Oral historians face the same dilemma when confronted with transcripts of conversations and interviews. The transcripts can capture all the words that were spoken, but grammatical markers such as commas and exclamation marks are poor substitutes for tone, rhythm, long pauses, and emotional swings in the speaker's voice.

When we listen to the noises and sounds of rural life, we can differentiate between the sawmill, whose noises had no direct social purpose but nevertheless conditioned social existence, and the ring of a church bell controlled by a higher authority. In the preindustrial era, church bells rang across the countryside of France to remind parishioners of the presence of God; the sound allowed the church to control the rhythm of its parishioners. When the church bells played the vespers, they were calling listeners to prayer and marking time. A minaret, absent the bells, had a similar function in the Muslim world—an official called from the top of the minaret at specific times of day to invite men for prayer. One cannot understand village life without recognizing these sounds.

In modern times, the sounds emanating from minarets have been recorded to play electronically from speakers, and church bells have been replaced with cassette recordings (the church across our street plays a cassette that garbles the bell sounds—perhaps a sign of economic recession within the religious community). These technologies are by no means recent inventions. Anyone who has taken a long elevator ride in the past 50 years is familiar with Muzak. Almost a century ago, authoritarian regimes understood the potential of piped music and lined streets with megaphones. The speakers were not posted on all streets, and it is difficult to determine when they were turned on and off, but they influenced the experience of residents. In *Feminine Frequencies: Gender, German Radio, and the Public Sphere, 1923–1945*, Kate Lacey cobbles together sources dealing with German radio and official attempts to steer the behavior of the women who listened to these transmitted sounds in the comfort of their homes. In a related vein, historians can interpret the significance of Soviet transistor radios that did not have tuner dials.

The phenomenon of producing sounds in public places is not unique to totalitarian governments. In the last century, citizens of modern democracies have become accustomed to music playing outside the elevator. In the United States, piped sounds were introduced in the 1930s and were explicitly designed to condition the mood of restaurant patrons. During World War II England introduced a "music while you work" campaign to lift the morale of factory workers and, in 1945, Waterloo Station welcomed its commuters with marching music. Although these experiments were short lived, background music quickly became ubiquitous in the social environment as entrepreneurs began to understand the economic benefits of piping sounds into public places.

At shopping malls music is played throughout the enclosed space and selectively in individual stores. Likewise, the sound profile at sporting venues has changed dramatically over the last half century. Whereas visitors to a Chicago hockey game in the 1970s listened to air traveling through the pipes of a grand old organ, modern spectators listen to rock music blasted at high volume. These sounds influence the human experience, form part of our history, and yet are rarely self-evident in written sources. Restaurant reviewers seldom mention sound profiles, and sports journalists ignore the artificial production of sound to focus on home runs and touchdowns. The sounds are particularly important in histories about the fate of marginalized people—individuals with hearing challenges are negatively impacted by an adverse sound environment just as the individual in a wheelchair is by a staircase.

The sound strategy at the mall is less obvious than that of communist regimes' street-side speakers. Nevertheless, we can try to understand the sound strategies employed, the social impact these sounds had, and how this impact has changed over time. Opera houses of the nineteenth century had a definite (nationalist and urbane) sound function. Today, stores play music to influence the moods of their shoppers in an effort to loosen purse strings. The sounds at the mall are therefore tied to the efforts of sociologists and psychologists who conduct research for malls. A store playing Muzak has to recover the cost of the service by raising prices. Restaurants play loud music to discourage their patrons from lingering. As with the church bells, the importance of the sounds extends well beyond the immediate impact on a human ear. In large venues such as sporting events, the production of sound intersects with corporate concerns. Organizers strike deals with music studios, thus the success of the music industry is linked to attendance at hockey games. The sounds might even be produced to prevent spectators from talking.

The modern examples are easier to consider as historical sources because the impact of sounds produced through loudspeakers seems obvious; for at least half a century, there have been many spaces—hospital rooms, commuter trains—where individuals simply could not escape the production of sound. At the very minimum, one can emphatically stress that no history of the world after 1950 will be complete without taking these sounds into consideration. Importantly, the overabundance of sound production in the modern age should not blind the historical researcher to exploring the dissemination of sound before the electrical reproduction of sound was possible.

Marc Raeff, a renowned historian of Imperial Russia, cautioned his colleagues to consider both the information in historical sources and the information purposefully omitted. When this caution is transposed into the world of sound, it reappears in this modified form: We must search for the sounds and noises of the past but also pay careful attention to silence. The world was and is a very noisy place, but sometimes silence has greater meaning. The first example is right under our noses (or next to our ears). Traditionally, the history professor conducted research in a quiet room in which she was not to be disturbed. What were the social ramifications of this silence? Did silence limit the accessibility of the profession since it discouraged potential historians who would have preferred a little chatter in the room? Since many young historians work with headphones, these historical questions about the profession are not irrelevant.

The impact of silence on the historical profession is not unique and has historical antecedents. The church of the Middle Ages is a particularly interesting example since clerical authorities valued silence. As they sought to transform the church from being a part of the world to a space apart from the world, they regulated activities within the walls of the church. Except for official ceremonies, the physical church was reformed into a quiet place. Brawling, markets, and trading were moved outside (much like smoking has been eliminated from most of our buildings) to make way for a more respectful atmosphere. The shift to less noise (or sometimes no noise at all) altered the behavior of individuals and is still in evidence today.

During the nineteenth century, the control of silence reflected a social strategy in the secular realm. Silence in the classroom was designed to produce educated but obedient children who would eventually serve state bureaucracies. Silence also became equated with the production of knowledge. The nineteenth century in Europe witnessed the growth of massive public museums. The museums were designed to advertise the scientific and cultural achievements of Europeans but also served to tame the behavior of the unruly classes. The educated elite encouraged the working classes to visit the museums, but they were expected to leave their loud, rowdy habits behind. In the silence of museum halls, they escaped industrial distractions and experienced the link between silence and knowledge. Silence became associated with soberness and intellectual investigation, quite the opposite environment of the corner pub. Other sites of silence, such as funerals, bear their own interpretive component.

Historically, then, trends in silence must be integrated into the analysis on the same terms as music, sound, and noise. Historians can make comparisons between silence in a church during a deeply religious age and silence in a museum during a secular, industrial, and urban period to link these findings to social and political issues. Did humans fear silence because it gave them more time to focus internally, an exercise Nietzsche suggested many humans were afraid to do? Or did silence bring greater societal order? The challenge for the historian, especially those focused on the pre-technological age, is to recognize these situations even though they may not be explicitly mentioned in sources—many written texts are silent about sound and also say nothing about silence.

Before ending with a few comments on traditional sources, we can pause to think about how a historian can use sources—once he has done due diligence and collected all this information. What possible complications arise when the historian has to balance oral and written testimony from contemporaries and subsequent accounts of the events? How can the questions we ask change our attitudes toward these sources?

The story of Kaspar Hauser, told in umpteenth variations since the early nineteenth century, highlights both complications in historical analysis and in the use of our favorite sources. Kaspar Hauser was an adolescent who suddenly appeared on the streets of Nuremberg, Germany, in May 1828. A local tradesman discovered him one morning in a town square. When the tradesman inquired into the young man's origins, Hauser did not respond in intelligible language. The only information he brought with him was found in a letter written in the anonymous hand of someone who claimed to be a day laborer. The letter did not give the exact details of his birth but it gave hints—he was born around the year 1812 near the Bavarian border, he had not been allowed outside the home since his birth, and he had been taught rudimentary aspects of writing and Christianity. As he adjusted to life in Nuremberg, Hauser added details to his story. In his own words, he had not been able to stand upright, had been locked in a dark room, and had been brought bread and water while he slept. His story immediately caught the attention of the local illuminati who seized upon it as an opportunity to examine the case of a half-wild man who had been raised outside of society. Logicians wanted to judge his capacity for reason, the clergy wanted to explore his understanding of God, and local residents wanted to attend the fair and gawk at this rare human specimen. Hauser spent a full five years in Nuremberg, where he not only acclimatized himself to urban living but underwent scores of tests and examinations by the curious. His role in the town was not uncontroversial as a masked man attacked him in 1829. The incident foreshadowed his eventual demise, because he was killed in another knife attack in December 1833 and died shortly thereafter.

The story of Kaspar Hauser, then and now, attracted massive amounts of attention precisely because his origins were unknown and unverifiable and opened the door to all sorts of fanciful storytelling. Was he the abandoned son of a princely house and thus a potential heir? Was he a charlatan who conned residents into believing his stories? Will DNA analysis allow researchers to answer all these questions? What advantages would be gained if we did have these answers? Should we even be concerned by the mix of oral and written sources that have convoluted this tale?

Posterity will probably be better off if it never discovers the "truth" about Kaspar Hauser, but the story demonstrates two different approaches to historical research. On the one hand, we can focus on discovering real facts about Hauser. On the other hand, we can use the story to develop a more complex understanding of life in Nuremberg in the 1830s. If we knew his birth story, we would be able to determine his relationship with a princely house and praise those who guessed best at his origins. If it came to light that a princely family had abandoned him, the new information would answer questions about the succession strategies of noble families in early nineteenth-century Germany.

The discovery of this information would not necessarily change our interpretation of the Nurembergers who lived with Hauser. Nevertheless, historians could study oral depositions, the notes of city officials, and the scribbling of the logicians to gain an understanding of the town as a whole. For example, all these sources can help us understand the lasting effects of the Enlightenment in a small German town almost 50 years after the height of Enlightenment thought. Did the methods of the logicians reflect rational thought in the town, or did their ideas represent the educated minority who were different from those who saw a witch in their midst? Independent of Hauser's own religious speculations, the depositions of villagers and town officials could indicate whether the town was entering into a more secular age that was representative of an urbanizing and industrializing society. When Hauser received help from townsfolk, do we see examples of Christian charity or a more secular form of philanthropy? The answers to these questions do not have to delve into Hauser's origins.

The meaning of the sources would undergo further transformation if a historian could convincingly demonstrate that specific residents in Nuremberg at the time had knowledge of Hauser's actual origins. If this were the case, the entire story of Kaspar Hauser would change because a contemporary would have knowingly manipulated the story. In this case, the historian could examine the motives for the manipulation and explain how the social setting in this town gave rise to a situation in which residents held secrets from each other and why other residents accepted stories they knew not to be true (the story of Martin Guerre in early modern France flows along these lines).

Unfortunately, in Hauser's time oral historians had yet to make their mark on the profession. Had oral historians been around, they would have collected sources more methodically through interviews with the residents. But even if an oral historian could magically conjure up an interview with an early nineteenth-century individual, the source would not be collected to uncover the simple truth about Hauser's birth. The oral historian would treat the source in a complex manner. For example, an oral historian would be interested to know how the passage of time altered the recollection of events. In other words, a Nuremberger's account of Hauser would change as additional experiences shifted an individual's memories of the events. Whether we draw our inspiration from Marcel Proust or Maurice

Halbwachs, historians now understand that memory is conditioned by intervening events. An elderly man can write about his high school days, but the account reflects the experiences of more than two discrete time periods (senior citizen and high school student). All the experiences that lay in between, from college student to young parent to middle-aged father, impact the construction of a memory in continual flux. Much like the example of the photograph of the German soldier taken in 1915, the quality of the memory will depend on the environment in which it is remembered. Each memory is refracted through a host of separate experiences.

Oral historians do not compile these sources to gather objective information about a past event. The oral historian collects narrative stories from individuals to get a better sense of a community's attitude and this individual's place within that community. A working-class individual or an African in London will filter memory through his communal experiences in the same way that the butcher in Nuremberg would interpret past events much differently from the scientific logician or the city councilor. Over the past 50 years, historians have more closely studied memories of foot soldiers, women behind enemy lines, and individuals whose experiences shed light on previously neglected topics. This is a vastly different enterprise from analyzing the memoirs of a famous general or politician like Gustav Stresemann mentioned earlier.

Let us now leave the final word to what is perhaps the most traditional and lasting of sources—the diary. After all the dynamic sources that have been presented, has the diary been pushed to the side of the road? Of course people still write private diaries, even in the age of Facebook, but are they static sources that can no longer be reconsidered, reworked, or reinterpreted? Traditionally, the diary is a private notebook with a mnemonic function for the writer. A diary can include secret codes or sublime symbols (such as the diary of the British iconographer Eric Gill, which had a system to note the positions in which he had had sex) to prevent outsiders from getting in. A famous diary like Anne Frank's can gain worldwide renown because it provides direct access to a global tragedy; the contrast between a child's innocence and the adult crimes of the Nazis engaged readers long after the war was over, the Nazis were defeated, and the author was deceased.

But diaries can reveal as much about contemporary society as they do about the author, and thus the diary as a source gains new meaning; it can become an object of public attention rather than a reflection of private thought. When published diaries have an immediate political impact, the actual contents can provoke wider debates that overshadow the original contents. In the early twentieth century, the Irish politician and nationalist Sir Roger Casement was convicted of treason. In an effort to muster support for his death sentence, the British government circulated parts of his diary. Readers were exposed to pages upon pages of lascivious writing describing the author's homosexual escapades with young men. Unwilling to accept these revelations from a well-respected man, his supporters defended the Irish hero and claimed the diary had been forged. Ultimately, the diaries were scientifically verified and little doubt remains about their veracity.

The controversy, however, reveals the complexity of the source. Once Casement's diary became public its nature as a historical source changed, for it no longer simply reflected the author's views at the time of its writing. Rather, it revealed a variety of societal views well after it had been written—attitudes that were not necessarily part of the diary itself. The diary was transformed into an object that exposed the values of British and Irish citizens. As an object, it became a prism through which to separate the values of contemporaries. Depending on the position individuals took with respect to the writing, it revealed the political and sexual leanings of segments of society in Ireland and Great Britain. As long as the diary continues to be read, it will retain this function. This is not to say that historians should forget about the author's original intentions. Rather, we should understand how a historical source can make the transition from intimate writing to public object. All sources are continually in transition and, whether visual, oral, object, or conventional, historians have to handle them with soft gloves.

In looking back at the terrain covered, many traditional sources have been slightly marginalized, though they still remain important. Antiquity has left archaeological objects of major significance. During the Middle Ages, churchmen left behind invaluable traces of intellectual and legal culture. When the modern European state of the seventeenth century superseded the church as the main administrative organ, it collected extensive data. State documents discuss laws, natural disasters, urban planning, religious conflict, censorship, and a whole range of relevant political issues. National archives now contain millions of files from current and defunct states, thus they still provide valuable information. The size of these collections should not, however, overshadow the opportunities offered by all the sources mentioned above.

Basically, anything that reveals itself to the five senses can be introduced into the historian's analysis. The challenge is to draw together this disparate set of sources and weave together a coherent narrative for readers and listeners. At times, the challenge is almost insurmountable because the historian has to look in so many unfamiliar places. Fortunately, however, historical research is to a large degree team oriented, and the historian relies on, and in her turn helps, a web of professionals who remove barriers, suggest new paths, and offer assistance. It is to this cooperative aspect of the historical profession that we now direct our attention.

Chapter 3

THE WEB OF THE HISTORIAN'S WORK

John Donne, the sixteenth-century English poet, wrote that "No man is an island, Entire of itself. Every man is a piece of the continent, A part of the main." Donne was emphasizing the communal spirit of human lives, but these thoughts also bear on historical scholarship. Our tradition of published monographs was designed to highlight a singular achievement and present the efforts of historians in isolation. In the process, the community of professionals whose expertise was instrumental in assisting the historian has become marginalized. Despite the importance of a variety of professions, numerous talented individuals get lost in the final product. Traditionally, the author of a monograph recognizes assistance from the outside in the acknowledgments, but this does not explain to the reader how this assistance took place.

For at least a generation, historians have been encouraged to take an interdisciplinary approach to their work, so there is already a sense of interaction with outsiders. But the term *interdisciplinary* suggests interactions with traditional university departments—sociology, economics, literature—and sidelines professions that do not fit comfortably into those departments. The term *interdisciplinary* therefore has limitations until we take into account the contributions of professionals whose work is not defined by a traditional academic discipline. The web of the historian can include a librarian at an academic library or at a small public library in a rural area, a curator at a museum, and even a trained gardener at a botanical garden. This web reveals how the specialties of one professional complement the specialties of the other.

Only thereafter, in the second half of this chapter, will we take a closer look at the interdisciplinary partners of the historian. The interdisciplinary methods take the historian well beyond the parameters of straightforward thought and integrate historical research into far-flung fields of philosophy and science. This second section serves two basic purposes: (1) It indicates how historians interact with other academic disciplines and highlights fruitful outcomes of these collaborations, and (2) it addresses the limits of interdisciplinary analysis, so newcomers to the field are not intimidated by the prospect of dabbling in science or philosophy.

In exploring these interactions, we should not forget that, more often than not, the friends of the historian have history degrees or have studied history. If we hold onto this idea for a moment, we take it in two directions. First, historical training has broad possibilities when students consider future career paths. The study of history can be paired with additional expertise in scores of institutional environments. Second, why should we not consider librarians or curators as full-scale historians in their own right? Why should we reserve the moniker "historian" to the narrow swath of professionals that reside in history departments when the title is subsumed in so many other activities? Is there such a thing as a pure historian? These are larger vocational questions that cannot find their full answer here. They can, nonetheless, draw additional attention to the importance of the historian's collaborators.

The cooperative web of the historian's work demonstrates how these professionals interact with historians; they are not simply handmaidens to the ultimate goal—that is, the single-authored monograph. The cooperation can be visualized as a series of Venn diagrams in which adjacent circles overlap but are never concentric. Librarians and curators assist historians, but this represents only a portion of their professional responsibilities. In turn, the historian assists the librarian or curator. In a previous chapter you saw that historians have limitless primary sources, but you did not experience how the historian gains access to these sources—access requires cooperation with specialists. When we think of the interactions on these terms, we avoid patronizing the efforts of adjacent professions, provide a better indication of the nature of cooperation, and expand on the well-intentioned comments in the acknowledgment sections of books.

We can begin by considering the librarian. A librarian has stereotypically been looked upon as a person who sits behind a desk, ready to respond to inquiries. The librarian makes the first-time visitor feel comfortable with the bookish environment until the initiate understands how to search for books; thereafter, he can dispense with the librarian's services. As a free soul, he can wander through the stacks and delight in the serendipity of discovering unknown little treasures stuck between dusty tomes—the good read that will make his day, month, and maybe even define his youth.

Despite the poetical waxing about stumbling upon unexpected books, most library stacks are well-ordered spaces that reflect the decisions of librarians who agonized about how to arrange the books on the shelves. Neither the Library of Congress system in American academic libraries nor the Dewey Decimal Classification popular in public libraries is accidental. Even when the historian believes she is roaming freely, the invisible hand of the librarian is mapping her route. In pessimistic circles, voices have suggested that the steering controls the production of knowledge, but that is a philosophical question for another time. Presently, the emphasis is on cooperation and the continued influence the librarian has on the books historians read.

The cooperation is much more than a function of reading books because the librarian pursues a host of activities that influence the outcome of research—the directed collection of books, the purchasing of older manuscripts, the development of search engines, collaboration on research projects, interlibrary loan systems, and the sharing of information. The digital library has radically altered the way professionals consider access to materials, but collaboration remains integral: Our libraries would exist without historians, but the historian could not exist without the library.

The collection of books ultimately determines what knowledge is stored within the physical and digital walls of the library. The original shelves were empty until a librarian with a budget decided to contact publishers, collectors, and editors. Depending on its priorities, each library develops its own collection. In conjunction with historians, scientists, and researchers, academic libraries complement a general collection with a focus on specific materials. For example, a library in Los Angeles can decide to place an emphasis on Spanish-language publications from past centuries. Bearing in mind that older books can be as precious as museum objects, the librarian responsible for acquisitions must be integrated within a web of antiquarian dealers who notify the library when rare materials become available. A copy of Vicente Tofiño de San Miguel's *Atlas Maritimo de Espana*, published in Madrid at the end of the eighteenth century, can be purchased for over $100,000.

The purchase of a single volume has broader intellectual ramifications for the host library and those who work there. An important research collection attracts specialists (physically or digitally) to the library. The collection puts the librarian at the heart of research inquiries from those who want to read the materials. Faced with a variety of requests, the librarian becomes the center of an exchange network directing the flow of research. Libraries regularly organize symposia to encourage assessments of their collections.

When we think of libraries we tend to think of long rows of books; when we think of museums we traditionally think of long rows of objects hanging on the wall or stored in glass cases. Both institutions have an academic air, but their missions are distinct. Museums tend to house physical objects that are meant to be viewed, whereas libraries hold billions of words hidden on the pages of books that are rarely opened. Because each institution has a distinct mission, each will attract a certain type of historian. Art historians are naturally attracted to traditional art museums, but because museums exist in such variety there is a museum for every historian. Moreover, since museums have been the depositories of historical artifacts for centuries, the range of artifacts is as diverse as the museums that store them. Classic examples express the importance of museum holdings. The Louvre in Paris is home to the *Mona Lisa*; the British Museum has the Elgin Marbles from Greece; the terracotta army of Qin Shi Huang is protected and preserved just east of Xi'an in China; the Smithsonian National Air and Space Museum in Washington, DC, houses artifacts of American aircraft innovation; and the Botanical Garden in Kolkata, India, has living examples of plants from around the world. A historian can examine portions of a museum's collection, consult a curator about the authenticity of an item, relate archaeological evidence to textual information, discuss changes to an artifact with a conservator, or co-produce an intriguing show for public consumption. All this research requires cooperation with a curator or conservator.

As an initial example we can look at a botanical garden, because it does not intuitively intersect with the concerns of the historian. What could the historian possibly want to know about plants and how could the curator/ gardener of a botanical garden be of assistance? Importantly, the movement of plants can help explain the ambitions and prejudices of European imperial powers. When European powers started to seek natural goods in the seventeenth century, they moved plants from one island to the next. Thus the plants around the world speak to the imperial practices of the European powers. In an Indian garden, the specialist can discuss the provenance (i.e., the hands through which the objects have passed) of the plants and how they came to be distributed throughout the world. The historical usage of each plant, as an economic or medical asset, offers keys to understanding trade patterns. The study of plants can also highlight the influences of Indian culture on the development of a European identity. Instead of marginalizing the contribution of Indian culture, it can be placed in the forefront. For example, what floral patterns in the textile industry were modeled on Indian plants? When the gardener explains original medical applications of the plant, this information reveals how local Indian medical practices affected European medical thought. Information on the productivity of wood or spices illuminates local agricultural practices. All this information needs to be collected in conjunction with plant experts.

The botanical garden is a bit of an exotic case of an outdoor museum; a more traditional example can extend the idea that historians cooperate with museum professionals. We have all visited museums stuffed with objects, but few of us recognize that what is actually on display represents only a small fraction of the museum's collection. Behind the public galleries of museums and tucked away in storage areas lie thousands upon thousands of carefully catalogued artifacts that few people ever see. To review this material, a historian must first consult with the curators to secure access. But it is not just a matter of getting permission to enter these secret chambers; the curator has her own interpretive tools to understand the objects, their provenance, and the changes they have undergone over time. For example, an art historian might look at a statue in storage to assess its beauty or position it within a specific art movement. For the social historian, the curators know where it was originally displayed (in a palace garden, a church, or a family's home) and can assist with questions about its physical influence in a social setting.

When curators trace the ownership of these objects, they help us to understand which social groups were interested in collecting and how these collections reflect the values of a social group. In the case of paintings or photographs, the museum staff has the necessary expertise to indicate retouching, the composition of the paint, as well as previous professional efforts to conserve the artifacts, such as the disastrous conservation techniques inflicted on the Elgin Marbles in the 1930s when conservators mistakenly whitened the marbles. The curator can interpret the actions of these conservators within the context of European science and its sense of exaggerated pride. These issues are difficult if not impossible for historians to address on their own.

Curators of photography are also valid team members. The complicated aspects of the source have been discussed in a previous chapter, but less was said about individuals who spend their professional lives with photographs. The curator alongside the historian can determine the chemical processes of a photograph to place photography within the history of science and technology. Curators can explain the exhibition history of photographs to provide clues about the historical status of photography as it was transformed from a means of technological reproduction to an art form. Many historians remain visually illiterate despite their much-vaunted reading aptitude. In contrast, the visual skills of the curator expand our understanding of basic visual impulses. The curator can also explain how the limitations of exposure times determined what images were taken and which moments the photographer had to ignore.

Curators are of course not the only employees at museums. The historian also interacts with conservators who repair, clean, and stabilize the artifacts; the trend to integrate unique sources of evidence will invariably increase the role of the conservator. Conservators can reveal clues about the layering of an artifact. Layers in an archaeological sense are familiar and easy to visualize—a team of researchers digs below the surface of the earth and the dig reveals layers of past civilizations (scientists in Antarctica do a similar experiment when they sample layers of ice). In a painting, the layers are less obvious because a top layer of paint conceals information below; to get at this information, a historian requires the techniques of the conservator.

The exhibition is another point of collaboration. Museum exhibitions gain renown for their popularity with the public, but they involve massive scholarly cooperations premised on a rethinking of a historical epoch or artistic style. In 2004, the Metropolitan Museum of Art in New York City opened an exhibition entitled *Byzantium: Faith and Power (1261–1557)*. The exhibition involved museums and specialists from around the world. Objects in the exhibition arrived on loan from Austria, Belgium, Egypt, France, Greece, Italy, Turkey, and a handful of other countries. In the exhibition catalogue, curators, librarians, conservators, philosophers, philologists, and historians contributed their knowledge to the relationship between Byzantine faith and fading Byzantine political power in the first half of the second millennium. The assembly of talent created a multidimensional perspective to study the Byzantine Empire. Not only did interested scholars have a chance to read essays about the Byzantine Empire, they could also visit the museum to pair three-dimensional objects with subtle narrative interpretations. A museum exhibition might even be considered the prototypical example of collaboration and the cross-fertilization of ideas.

Museums are also sites of collection and preservation; someone has to decide what to preserve and historians benefit from these decisions (or lose out when a museum has no additional storage space). The story of a man in Central Asia illustrates the importance of collection at both the personal and institutional level. Igor Savitsky, born in 1915, attended art school in Moscow, but when World War II came he was temporarily evacuated to Central Asia with scores of Soviet citizens. After the war he returned to Central Asia, where his focus eventually shifted from painting to collecting cultural artifacts of Karakalpakstan, an autonomous region in the Soviet republic of Uzbekistan. Miraculously, he managed to secure funding from local communist officials to build the premises for his collection. At the same time, he assembled works from avant-garde artists in Moscow whose works were hidden and decaying because the regime preferred socialist realism to the avant-garde of the 1920s. Defying the censors, he went to Moscow where he visited the homes and studios of artists (and their children) to procure works for the museum in Uzbekistan. He spent state funds, his own funds, or wrote IOUs to the recipients. He then rolled up the canvasses and traveled back to Karakalpakstan. By 1966 he had collected enough art to open a museum in Nukus, the capital of the region. According to estimates, he managed to collect around 80,000 pieces before his death in 1984, and since the collapse of the Soviet Union parts of the collection have been displayed in museums in Chemnitz, Germany, and Caen, France.

The larger theme in this story is the fragility of objects and collections. In Savitsky's case, the political circumstances placed serious hurdles in the way of preserving the past. But he did not just collect art—he had to preserve it. Preservation is a continual concern for curators and historians. Savitsky, for example, could not predict the collapse of the Soviet Union. When the Soviet Union did collapse in 1991, the collection found itself in a peculiar geopolitical environment: Although the painted art had come overwhelmingly from Moscow, the museum was now outside the borders of the Russian Federation. Could Uzbekistan provide enough funding to store the art in the proper climatic conditions? In tumultuous political times, who would have the resources to protect the artwork from predatory international art thieves who keep abreast of weaknesses in the museum edifice as they plan their next heist? Would the Russian families of the artists call in the IOUs now that the art could fetch millions in an open market? Scholars had to unite to protect the integrity of the collection. This theme is not unique to the museum in Nukus. A Hollywood film has recently been made, *The Monuments Men*, about scholars who went to Europe to protect art once the Nazis had lost control of an area. After the American invasion of Iraq, the National Library and Archive was intentionally set aflame; again, teams of scholars are involved in resurrecting the remnants of collections.

Besides the political uncertainties, Savitsky's collection rises and falls with interpretive trends among historians. In 1998, Stephen Kinzer wrote about the museum for the *New York Times* and suggested that a chapter in art history may have to be rewritten. The collection *might* change interpretations of avant-garde art or, alternatively, it could confirm what we already know. If Savitsky collected pieces of art that bore a resemblance to standard pieces of the avant-garde, then the collection will be perceived as less revolutionary. In this case, the chapter in art history won't have to be rewritten because it will suffice to add footnotes here and there to confirm rather than radically change prior interpretations. In the extreme, future generations *might* forget about the collection altogether. The museum would share the fate of Ozymandias, the king of kings, whose mighty works were swallowed by sand. Whatever happens in the future, Savitsky's instinct of preservation performed a great service for artists and historians.

Much emphasis in this book has been placed on the traveling historian. Savitsky's story reminds us how far and wide objects can travel before they land in front of the historian—it is as if there were two moving targets. But bureaucratic documents travel just as well as avant-garde art. In 1941, the Nazi army captured the Soviet city of Smolensk and the archive of the Communist Party in that city. Because the archive contained such valuable information, the Nazis moved part of the archive to Vilnius in Lithuania and a portion to Bavaria. When the Nazis were defeated, American intelligence officers got their hands on the Bavarian files and transported the files back to the United States, where American historians made good use of them. The materials were only returned to the Russian Federation in 2002. The more these documents move about, the more important the collectors become.

An archivist can also be subsumed under the broader definition of the collector. In a more formal and larger institutional setting, archivists determine the documents to collect. Archivists actively pursue materials—such as the personal diaries of a philosopher, the photographs of an important artist, the correspondence of a soldier, or the documents pertaining to a marine expedition—and have a fundamental bearing on the preservation and further dissemination of these materials. Aided by the tenets of archival science, they order the documents and present meaningful descriptions of document collections. Without the overview of the archivist, the historian would be lost.

Decisions on how to present the material to visitors of the archive are no less essential. The archivist has to decide how to categorize materials. For example, an archive can continue the original ordering of government files, as suggested in an earlier chapter. If the Department of the Interior of the United States was divided into specific subdepartments and field houses, the archive can order the material accordingly. A historian interested in Native American issues can request historical documents from the Bureau of Indian Affairs and will receive the documents just as the bureau had organized and filed them.

Alternatively, an archive can sort documents according to associations, political parties, specific media outlets, or as an assemblage of personal documents from a famous individual. Each archive will have its own policy, but individual classification techniques mean the researcher will come across the documents in unique contexts. Two exact copies of a letter can appear in two separate sections of an archive—in a ministerial folder and in the personal file of an individual collection. Let us say the letter came from a revolutionary whose activities were a threat to the state. In the ministerial folder, the researcher will come across official discussions that highlight the danger of the individual and the successful state attempts to limit this individual's activity. In the personal files, the letter can be part of a correspondence with fellow revolutionaries who laud and complement each other's activities. The context in which this letter is read will affect the interpretation—a historian who is only aware of the documents placed in the police file can misjudge the influence state surveillance had on the revolutionaries. If you read only the correspondence of the revolutionaries, you risk getting an exaggerated sense of their activities. The meaning depends on the context in which the document is read—much like the beauty of the ugly duckling depended on the friends he kept.

Archives assist researchers with this context by developing navigational tools. Much like a table of contents has a navigational purpose, archival roadmaps offer a way to explore vast collections. These roadmaps influence the likelihood of certain documents getting attention—when a cartographer decides to leave out roads and alleyways on a map, cars are less likely to explore those streets. The finding aids, for example, list the titles of documents and give brief descriptions of the collection. The titles give a broad indication of what the file contains, but titles can only superficially touch upon the contents. More importantly, the titles steer research.

In the good old days, the historian read through thousands of titles in awkward handwriting (made even more difficult when the handwriting was in Cyrillic or Arabic) to select documents worth examining. The process was simplified with typed lists, and now databases can be searched at site or online. Instead of reading lists, keyword searches now lead the researcher to files of interest. The databases change the nature of inquiry much like searching an electronic library catalogue eliminates random acts of finding books in the stacks. With the keyword searches, the researcher sees all titles with the search term but remains unaware of adjacent files that might contain equally important information, just under another name.

The file names only touch upon the contents, but they have a vast influence. When men dominated the political world, files were named according to themes of interest to these men. A scholar interested in pursuing the career of a woman would not have direct access to the necessary files. In the case of correspondence, the researcher has to concoct indirect search strategies. Archives tend to file letters under the name of the famous person (in the past usually a man) in whose possession the letters were found. This system privileges the recipient of the letter but not the person who wrote the letter. The names of women who wrote these letters will not appear in a keyword search unless the researcher knows to whom these women were writing their letters.

Archives have other means to steer the search procedures. For example, an archive can emphasize process over product, or product over process. In the first case, the archivist prepares a written overview of a collection to indicate its contents for the viewer. This initial processing filters out files of little interest to a research agenda, though the historian has to rely on the thoroughness of the archivist. If the product has precedence over the process, the historian enters the archival city without a map, so to speak. Documents are available much quicker but without the assurance of oversight. In the finding aids of the National Archives and Records Administration in Riverside, California, researchers can locate categories of documents that are stored in boxes, but there is little information about the contents of the boxes. This places a greater burden on the researcher—but then searching and searching again is part of the job description. Fortunately, this exploration has a collaborative component because readers of the documents assist in the archive's own process of self-discovery. Since many documents rarely get carefully screened, the random requests from researchers help archivists build knowledge about their own collections.

The National Archives and Records Administration, the US federal depository on the far edge of Los Angeles, is worth a few more words. Set in an extremely arid, agricultural landscape that is far removed from urban centres, the regional archive holds documents from southern California, Arizona, and Clark County, Nevada; it represents a cog in a larger federal scheme with branches spread throughout the United States. The archive holds documents from federal field offices in its designated region. Importantly, the archive has extensive files from the Bureau of Indian Affairs, located within the US Department of the Interior. It does not, however, have documents from the State of California unless the documents interacted with the federal bureau. Researchers who want information from state bureaus have to visit the appropriate state archives.

Although the location of the archive hardly encourages drop-in visitors, the archivists deal with requests that are not linked with the efforts of professional historians. Genealogists, for example, have a role every bit as important as the historian. When plans were in the making to close the Georgia Archives to the public, the Georgia Genealogical Society exerted pressure to keep them open. At Riverside, genealogists work together with archivists to piece together family histories. In addition to the genealogists, archivists work together with representatives of Native American tribes and a range of lawyers and attorneys. Native American tribes have their own archival collections but need to visit the federal archives to rectify enrolment issues within the tribe.

Since researchers can be covetous about their sources as they hope for the next breakthrough, an unspoken Hippocratic oath exists between the historian and the archivist. To respect the privacy of researchers, the archivists don't pass on information about individual researchers' requests and researchers names do not appear on the documents they have consulted (in contrast to Russian archives, where users identify themselves on all files they read). This privacy issue is not a hindrance to collaboration, for historians and archivists work together on issues such as document retention. Even in a digital age, an archive cannot store every single piece of information; the information would be impossible to catalogue and index. Historians, however, can help archivists identify files and documents of interest. For example, the archive cannot store all court cases, but historians can identify seminal court cases and cases that highlight general legal trends. Coming from outside the archive, they have a unique perspective on the events. Then historians and archivists can consult on the retention schedules for the documents, that is, how long the archive should actually hold on to the material.

In the state of Texas, the Harry Ransom Center has a large collection of archived objects and advertises its efforts to preserve materials. In the process, it offers precious insights into the difficult decisions archivists have to make. With the advent of the digital age, the Center has confronted the complicated transition from paper to digital collections. While it might appear straightforward to scan documents, originals from the nineteenth century were not designed for the scanner. In 1819, Elizabeth Barrett Browning wrote a poem called *The Battle of Marathon*. As the Center explains, the poem was written in iron gall ink and the pages were bound together with "irregular sewing." The sewing embodies social and gender aspects of the early nineteenth century, and thus the importance of the sewing cannot be overlooked when archiving the poem. To add another layer of complexity, the author wrote her edits on a separate piece of paper and then sewed the revisions over the old text, thus blocking the original text underneath. The physicality of the poem and the marks of the stitches were integral to the poetic work, yet the digital viewer needed access to the revised and unrevised text. Somehow the poem had to be pulled apart, scanned, and then reassembled.

The decision was made to remove one side of the sewing so that the new text could be lifted up to permit a digital scan of the original text underneath; the new text could then be sewn with "archival thread that was a close match to the original thread used by the author." This procedure was painful and still unsatisfactory because it compromised the physicality of the document. It was then decided to reuse the original thread. The conservator developed a diagram to track the sewing pattern since the stitches sometimes passed through three pages. The conservators retained the spirit of the original although, as the Center admits, it had to make certain cuts in the thread, and the knots Browning carefully tied could not be reproduced exactly. Is the document any less interesting or iconic because the knots have been shifted? Probably not, but the intricate process highlights the complex decision making of preparing materials before they reach the visitor in the reading room.

The Harry Ransom Center also makes decisions on acquisitions. In the same newsletter in which it explained the sewing dilemma it reported on its acquisition of the papers of Peter Orlovsky, an American poet associated with the Beat Generation. The collection has photographs, correspondence, notebooks, and additional items that intersect with the interests of important Beat poets and novelists. As a depository of Beat literature, the Center can develop into a focal point of innovation and discussion, physically in Austin and digitally throughout the world, thus leading research efforts.

The previous two examples stress the academic mission of the Harry Ransom Center, but it would be unfair to leave the discussion there. It is not only a meeting point for scholars of the Beat Generation but a transitional zone where public and academic interests meet. The bulk of the archival materials remain in storage, but efforts are made to publicize the collection. The Center has interactive computer kiosks where visitors can explore the Gutenberg Bible from the fifteenth century or examine the first photograph by Joseph Nicéphore Niépce from the start of the nineteenth century. A visitor can make a virtual heliograph that replicates Niépce's original technique; this image can then be sent as an email, a much easier digital reproduction than Browning's poem.

Major archives such as the Ransom Center have trained professionals who oversee vast collections. Not all archives, however, have the luxury of paid staff. In local historical societies, the preservation of works depends on local volunteers. These volunteers have an active interest in preserving the local record but do not always contextualize the local record within national affairs or have the resources for intricate sewing projects. The city of Breteuil, for example, has a historical society founded in 1984. Breteuil, a small town about 100 kilometers north of Paris, might be a strange place to visit for historical information, but it was the birthplace of Hippolyte Bayard, a pioneer of photography from the early nineteenth century. Bayard, a bureaucrat by day and dabbler in photography in his free time, is of particular interest to the town because of his association with the early days of technical reproduction through photography. A researcher can contact the historical society to procure information about the photographer.

This investigative approach differs from the one used in larger archives. Since the historian is probably located in Paris for the bulk of her research, arrangements have to be made to make the trip to Breteuil. Unlike the comparatively anonymous experience of researching in a larger archive, smaller archives have a more personal touch. If a trip is carefully planned, a member of the historical society might pick up the historian at the train station and shuttle her to the local archive; introductions can be made in the car. While reading documents, a friend of mine eavesdropped on the board meeting of the historical society because it took place in the same room at the same time; members discussed items such as biographies of local bishops or an exhibition featuring old photographs of the construction of the train station. The historical society has access to thousands, not millions, of documents to piece together this local history.

The local archivists, historians, and volunteers can position a historical inquiry relative to a specific local question. For example, local data can be instructive in highlighting the network of local friends and relatives in which Bayard was raised. While the historical society will have insights into these questions, it does not have keys to all doors. A careful researcher will note the overlap between documents in local and national archives. The material in archives in historical societies is often not a local product but the result of material gathered and copied from national and church archives. Moreover, these materials require contextualization in broader scenarios, scenarios that the larger collections in Paris will provide. The sheer size of Parisian archives should not, however, undermine the importance of collaborating with the volunteers at a local historical society such as the one in Breteuil. At the very least, it gives the historian a better understanding of the physical landscape of provincial France, something that the streets of Paris are ill equipped to do.

The last few pages have been written with an eye on the interaction between historians and archivists. But archivists, who are independent professionals, only spend a portion of their time with historians. We should therefore take a quick look at the more humorous demands random individuals place on archivists; this gives an even more dynamic sense of archival activity. In an entertaining and enlightening artistic video called *Photograph of Jesus* (2008), Laurie Hill has documented the trials and tribulations of an archivist who oversees the Hulton Archive in England (formerly known as the Hulton Picture Library and now part of Getty Images). The seven-minute clip takes a video camera deep into this visual archive and presents the viewer with a collage featuring long rows of dusty boxes, card files, select photographs from the 1800s, filing cabinets, and white gloves. (You can find the video at YouTube by searching the title.) As the video artist weaves this visual tale, an employee of the archive narrates his experiences with users.

The archive contains visual materials from the birth of photography in the 1830s. Because of its age, users expect it to have everything. The archivists thus receive comical requests in the form of insurmountable challenges such as an inquiry for a photograph of Jesus. Needless to say, Jesus was born well before the invention of photography—so how could the archive provide a photograph of Jesus? Toward the end of Hill's video, a photograph of Jesus does appear on the screen. As the camera pulls away to present the full context, the viewer sees a very modern collage with a happy American family in the foreground and the Jesus figure walking on water in the background. Another visitor requested a photograph of Jack the Ripper but, as the archivist relates, if they did possess a copy it would solve the most famous unsolved crime in history. If they had a photograph of a yeti, they would make buckets of money. And how should they have responded to the individual who requested a photograph of Adolf Hitler from the 1948 London Olympics? Or to the woman who wanted a photograph of Neil Armstrong and the 12 other astronauts who were on the moon with him? When the request came in for a photograph of a dodo, the archivist had to know that the dodo bird was extinct before the invention of photography.

But as the narrator adds, the archive contains so much material that, against all odds, it might contain a photograph of a yeti or Jack the Ripper. The archive has no exact figures for its collection but reckons that it contains 60 million images with thousands of boxes that the archivists have never been through. Therein lies the excitement and again the need for cooperation with outside users. The archivists require these requests to push them deeper into the dark recesses of the archive, or "Aladdin's Cave," to use the words of the narrator. An ongoing dialogue (or a trialogue) exists between the archivist, the user, and the object. The search for the yeti photograph could inadvertently reveal unseen images of the Tibetan highlands. The archivist also draws a parallel with the game of telephone to express how users come to hear about the collection. As word about the archive is passed around, the message gets subtly changed to the point where individuals come to expect that the archive has every imaginable photograph at its fingertips.

Surprisingly, archivists who tell jokes at their users' expense point us back to an earlier theme—historical researchers depend on other professionals to locate exotic yet necessary materials. Without librarians, curators, archivists, and other professionals, historians would keep writing the same books. The interpretive and professional web is complex but has to be recognized since its ultimate value rarely appears in published works. And what is that ultimate value? The research brings together curious individuals with different interests to solve common problems.

Many historians may be introverts and quiet souls who prefer solitude to the madness of crowds, but they do not work in isolation. They depend on collegial relationships with other professionals; each group has its own role to play in the reconstruction of the past and in steering the manner in which the past is studied. Without the librarian, the historian would have fewer books; without the archivist, the historian would have few documents to leaf through. Even governmental agencies that supply reports or perspectives to the historian affect the manner in which historians do their work. It is not necessary to determine the exact influence of each group as long as we remember that many actors have a role to play and the importance of this role changes with the circumstances. The historian is continually moving from place to place in this professional web.

The discussion so far has tried to shed the bookish image of the historian and scholar, and instead of referencing textbooks and scholarly monographs it has highlighted the multifaceted aspects of historical research. While all that activity has been brought to the fore, we should not overlook the importance of traditional work—historians must still read the works of fellow historians at their desks or at the coffee shop. There is, however, a twist to this part of the chapter. Instead of looking at how historians read the works of their colleagues the discussion below focuses on historians who have reached out to scholars whose works would not immediately suggest an interest in the study of the past. Over the years, historians have become increasingly aware of the benefits of this interdisciplinary approach. Although it involves trial and error as well as the risk of failure, an interdisciplinary attitude can lead to unexpected conclusions. Interdisciplinary historians can adopt visual, musical, philosophical, statistical, and medical approaches to answer intriguing questions.

Presenting these approaches is difficult because they necessarily veer off in all directions. The only thing that links the historians below is the fact that they all introduced methods from outside the historical discipline. It is difficult to keep track of this diversity, so two preliminary thoughts are in order. First, the reader should focus on the sheer variety rather than getting tripped up in the details. Second, it should be clear that even the most dedicated historian will have a hard time deciphering these methods because not all historians are trained in all disciplines. It should hardly be surprising if the lay reader (and the lay reader is often the historian) struggles with this interdisciplinary network of ideas.

The first section looks at four interdisciplinary historians. Carl E. Schorske examined Vienna, the cultural capital of the Germanic world, from a *visual* and *musical* perspective to grasp its transformation from a noble city into a modern bourgeois cultural center. Paul Veyne adopted relativist *philosophical* views to question if Greeks of antiquity, famous for their myths, actually bought into those myths. In an innovative military history,

John Komlos gathered massive *statistical* evidence to evaluate the health of soldiers in the Habsburg Empire at the end of the eighteenth century; the analysis never touched on the military performance of soldiers. William H. McNeill, a pioneer in the field of world history, merged the *biological* concept of the parasite with the process of colonization.

The second section looks at two nonhistorians who nonetheless did historical work and influenced the research of historians. In numerous cases, individuals trained in science and philosophy have tried their hands at analyzing the past and have written influential histories. Jared Diamond, a geographer, developed theses that have a growing influence in historical circles. His geographical histories have premises worth exploring. From a philosophical and sociological perspective, Jürgen Habermas wrote a critique of the bourgeois public sphere that had a deep influence on how historians conceptualized public activity. Although historians pay much less attention to Habermas's philosophical works, his historical analysis of the bourgeoisie readily shows how a mix of philosophy and history can motivate new directions in historical analysis.

In 1981, Schorske's *Fin-de-Siècle Vienna: Politics and Culture* won the Pulitzer Prize for General Nonfiction. As the home of Sigmund Freud, Gustav Klimt, and Arnold Schoenberg, Vienna was an obvious choice to study, though the choice of this city did not predetermine the method. In his introduction, Schorske expressed concern that academic disciplines had become too independent of each other. He referred to a multidisciplinary approach to describe his effort to reach out beyond the traditionally conceived confines of an academic discipline. Schorske applied this method when he explored the link between the demise of liberal political dreams and the emergence of new cultural movements. The artists and authors studied by Schorske had been raised in a liberal tradition, but they broke away from liberalism and became active agents in its demise. In the Ringstrasse of the middle of the nineteenth century, Schorske saw the expression of bourgeois and liberal values—in museums and the university—but these values were challenged by the end of the nineteenth century. In music, composers abandoned compositional schemes associated with the city's liberal period.

Art, architecture, and music thus lead the multidisciplinary way. In his essay "Explosion in the Garden: Kokoschka and Schoenberg," Schorske paralleled the atonality of Schoenberg's music with the demise of liberal rationalism. Schoenberg exited his own place in the bourgeois order and entered an atonal world that defied singular categorization. Schoenberg's atonality revealed a chaotic world teeming with atomized individuals. In the wake of Schoenberg, a composer could mix and match tones to his liking. Schorske likens this post-liberal phenomenon to the German proverb "Wer die Wahl hat, hat die Qual" ("He who has choice has torment"). In the late nineteenth century, the challenge was to exploit such diverse possibilities.

So far a lay reader without musical training, such as this author, can follow the multidisciplinary adventure. But Schorske's analysis pushes deeper into musical terrain. In Schoenberg's song cycle *The Book of the Hanging Gardens*, Schorske indicates devices that express its atonality. He writes that in the piano introduction, "[r]hythm crosses the bar line, ignores the meter—a free pattern of quarter notes—first four, then two, then five, before they sweep upward and subside again. . . . A tone will break into a privileged position, but disappear again into the mass, like a stone cast into the dark pond." These references will be difficult for the casual reader to comprehend.

If the lay reader (the historian of politics, economics, or architecture) cannot decipher the atonalities, the historian of music can weigh in with words of expertise. In a review from the early 1980s, a musicologist criticized Schorske's presentation of Schoenberg as an enemy of the tonal world. Instead, the reviewer responded that Schoenberg mixed lucidity and obscurity but paid deep respect to his tonal forefathers insofar as the tonal and atonal processes in music have parallels. The multidisciplinary historian is definitely vulnerable to critiques from the home discipline, but Schorske's approach brings together subdisciplines of the historical profession. In concert, they can reconsider basic principles in light of Schorske's masterful weaving together of threads. And even if the music must remain silent for many educated readers, Schorske demonstrates how the bourgeois vision of the future collapsed in face of this multidimensional charge.

Four years after Schorske, Paul Veyne tempted his readers with a simple title: *Did the Greeks Believe in Their Myths?* The answer was yes, but the author wanted to do more than confirm what everyone already knew. To this end, Veyne embedded his historical discussion in philosophical notions popular in the 1970s. He blended philosophy and history to answer his title question in a philosophical spirit. Philosophically, Veyne relied on the idea that facts, rather than representing the bedrock of analysis, are extremely ambiguous. Friedrich Nietzsche had argued that we are trained to believe truths, thus the value of truth lies in social habits. Truth then is not a static category for timeless assertions but a moveable target dependent upon circumstances. Truths were not awaiting to be discovered in nature or presented to us by an external force but born in what Veyne called the *constitutive imagination*—the human imagination was the most potent ingredient.

Myths were conducive to an analysis based on these ideas because myths are ambiguous. On the one hand, scholars point out that in ancient societies myths were effective because people in pre-rational periods believed in them hook, line, and sinker. After the Enlightenment and the promotion of rationality, the rational citizen wondered at the naiveté of past civilizations when it seemed so easy to separate the real from the mythical. All an individual had to do was put any myth to the test of reason. In contrast, Veyne argued that once the constitutive imagination went to work, it was no longer that easy to separate the real from the mythical. Veyne blended philosophy and history to explain Greek attitudes to their myths; his playfulness added ambiguity to historical interpretation.

His book examined social conditions and historical contingencies that determined attitudes toward these myths. A single individual could both believe and reject myth. The second-century physician Galen, for instance, straddled the world of belief and disbelief. In his medical writings, he refuted the existence of centaurs and thought it childish to focus on such nonentities as the centaur's bile. But when Galen sought new disciples, he happily leaned upon the supernatural and felt comfortable ascribing a historical role to none other than the centaur Chiron. Galen adopted this rhetorical ploy to convince his followers. Nevertheless, Galen slipped effortlessly from the world of the nonbeliever to the world of the believer. As Veyne wrote, "exploring minds have different aims and tactics, depending on the circumstances." In these cases, our grip on reality is loose indeed.

In linking truth with social class, Veyne demonstrated how the elite manipulated myths depending on their needs. If it served their best interests, they had their genealogy linked in such a way that it originated among the gods. In Plato's *Lysis*, the young boy had an ancestor who was related to Zeus. In other circumstances, talk about titans and giants was censored. In Aristophanes's *The Wasps*, a son discouraged his father from talking about myths because it was impolite to mention them at the table. The behavior met with disapproval because talk about myths was associated with the lower classes. Despite the suspicious approach of the elite, myths remained popular among the masses (although Veyne provided the example of a doubting slave). These variances are significant because no single version enjoys higher ground or has a stronger claim to truth.

From our vantage point 2,000 years later, when centaurs have long since been relegated into the realm of the fictional, we might question why myths are still worth the attention Veyne gave them. His words have significance because they demonstrated how contemporary philosophical thoughts can bring their weight to bear on the interpretation of distant historical epochs. Veyne employed his philosophical toolbox to emphasize how individuals and societies could hold seemingly contradictory beliefs. He also demonstrated that each individual or society molds truth to its needs.

Veyne's ideas were inspired by continental philosophy of the 1970s and applied to Greek storytelling. This winding route links isolated scholarly areas. The route to science, however, does not have to be as circuitous, and historians have taken direct inspiration from science, bypassing philosophy altogether. In 1977, William McNeill wrote *Plagues and Peoples* and explored how diseases affected the development of human civilizations. McNeill argued that parasitic epidemics had a dramatic impact on human history across the globe. He did not simply graph the deadly effects of disease but studied the transmission of disease and the immunities societies developed against them. Perhaps the most significant conclusion was that the Spanish success in the New World was not a function of Spanish military superiority, religious enlightenment, or intellectual advancement. Rather, victory came as a result of the diseases the Spaniards unwittingly brought with them and for which the native populations had absolutely no immunity. Given the Spaniards' ignorance of epidemiology, they were (wilfully) blind to the reasons for their own success. A key to the interpretation was McNeill's willingness to read medical journals, the *Bulletin* of the World Health Organization, and existing histories of medicine to enhance the interdisciplinary aspect of his research. This was a radical departure from the traditional sources employed to explain the Spanish conquest of the Americas.

The emphasis on medicine and medical history led to other interesting directions. For example, McNeill discussed microparasites. Microparasites are the bacteria and viruses, invisible to the naked eye, that seek human hosts. They can kill the human host, use the host as a carrier before finding more fertile ground, or establish a stable relationship with the host. Throughout much of human history, the host had little knowledge of the microparasites' activities.

The emphasis on the micro changed the way history has been told. It shifted the locus of action away from human beings and onto the little parasites that humans accidentally carried. Instead of attributing the rise and expansion of Europe to ingenious Europeans, McNeill turned the attention of his readers to contingencies that were not based on a premeditated rational plan. Thus, it was an accident that Europeans gained immunity to diseases. This accident, however, prompted population growth, encouraged travel, and germinated other social and political trends. Even when Europeans recognized the presence of disease, human intervention could only do so much. The Venetians in the fifteenth century had a basic understanding of quarantine and required potential plague-bearing ships to anchor away from the harbor for a period of time. Despite these active measures, the transmission of diseases went ahead without direct European intervention.

More important than the reduction of disease was the growing immunity Europeans had to disease. Since Europeans had such extensive exposure to all sorts of parasites, by the time they were adults they were much less susceptible to microparasites. This immunity—the result of centuries of travel, exploration, and exposure to different human populations—conditioned European expansion. In contrast, the populations in the New World had had very little exposure to diseases and had not had an opportunity to develop immunity. The Europeans did not know about the microparasites they bore with them, but "trifling" diseases of the Old World became deadly killers when they arrived in South America. Ultimately, diseases killed up to 90 per cent of local populations. Given the destruction, it was understandable that even the local population believed God was on the side of the Spaniards.

A thesis about the accidental or contingent nature of history can appear fragile in light of the known role of European armies, universities, and theological doctrines—it seems fanciful to suggest these complex human forces were handmaidens to microparasites. Nevertheless, the interdisciplinary approach cautions against human hubris and rightfully argues that even if epidemiological phenomena are not solely responsible for the unfolding of history they deserve consideration as part of the explanation. The epidemiological approach has also challenged the traditional Eurocentric attitude to writing history and encouraged a more global understanding of history. Historians refer to a Eurocentric approach to describe historical narratives that place the actions of Europeans at the center. In these histories, the Europeans create history while the conquered or colonized peoples around the globe submit passively to the will of the representatives of an advanced civilization. Over the years, historians have become dissatisfied with this approach because it categorically ignores the strategies of native populations and effectively silences their voices. Although McNeill focused on European sources and was less determined to write the history of local populations than many of his contemporaries, his epidemiological approach took the wind out of the Europeans' sails. He refused to ascribe European successes to Eurocentric characteristics, and in so doing he opened the way for historians to explore areas in which Europeans were less dominant than once thought. Furthermore, the ample use of medical terminology in *Plagues and Peoples* testifies to the crossover between the interests of medical science and history. The historian will never discover a cure for a disease, but McNeill integrated societal values and medicine so that the two fields can work together when the next crisis arises.

McNeill was just one of many historians to engage in scientific analysis. In 1989 John Komlos published *Nutrition and Economic Development in the Eighteenth-Century Habsburg Monarchy*. This creative work combined medical history, statistical analysis, mathematical formulae, and economics to draw conclusions about the state of Austrian society at the onset of the Industrial Revolution. Komlos referred to his method as *anthropometrics*, the study of measurements as related to human beings. Komlos integrated ideas from historians who had explored similar methods before computers could process data sets that ran into the hundreds of thousands. A generation earlier, Emmanuel Le Roy Ladurie had already made a correlation between the height of French recruits and their ability to read. In the late 1840s, literate French recruits were on average 1.2 centimeters taller than illiterate recruits. These were averages so they do not exclude the possibility that a tall recruit was illiterate or that a short recruit could read Voltaire.

Drawing inspiration from this method, Komlos proposed a direct correlation between height and the state of the economy; with sufficient data on growth patterns, historians can draw conclusions about the standard of living. Komlos therefore looked at the height of soldiers, because the army collected excellent data on its soldiers when other statistics were either unavailable or only spottily recorded. In the absence of other data, height is an effective indicator because it embodied many aspects of economic wealth. Weight was also an important measure but varied more than height over the lifetime of an individual, thus reliable statistics are harder to come by.

Height indicated cumulative nutrition over the growing years of an individual, evinced information about the nutritional status of the mother, and provided evidence about the degree of nourishment the individual received in his first two decades. If a population increased in average height, the historian can conclude that it had an improving food supply, which in turn suggests that the population had an increasing standard of living—economic prosperity is reflected in human growth. This data cannot reveal the composition of the diet or the effect of cultural habits on caloric intake, but it approximates the general well-being of the population.

Since Komlos considered several factors, he employed mathematical formulae to quantify variables that influenced the stature of Habsburg subjects. The formula below, difficult for anyone trained in the humanities to comprehend, is presented not to confound the reader with a mathematical challenge but to symbolize the range of methods used to interpret past events. The equation represents the terminal height of a population. The variables are defined as follows: height (H), time (t), tastes (T), income (Y), food costs (Z), and claims on nutrients (W):

$$H = H_{min} + \int_{t=-1}^{t=25} [g(Y_t, Z_t, T, W_t, t)]dt \leq H_{max}, \quad (1.4)$$

The formula, only one in a series of equations, suggests the mathematical complexity of the historical analysis and explains the relationship between the economy and human stature. Importantly, it indicates how a historian needs to cooperate with computer experts to compute the data.

After assembling data from thousands of government documents and featuring them in charts, tables, and graphs, is it enough to demonstrate that stature stabilized at the end of the eighteenth century, or is there more to the story? Komlos reinserted his statistics into larger issues by relating the height of individuals to the living conditions fostered by the Industrial Revolution—this is a huge mental jump, but the method makes it possible. In contrast to many scholars, Komlos argued that the onset of the Industrial Revolution did not immediately impoverish the masses of people who lived in cities. Instead, he argued that industrialization emancipated peasants from poverty because it slowed the shrinking of stature. Historians can disagree with this conclusion with the use of other historical methods, but here we just want to recognize the innovative technique. While many historians could hardly be concerned with a centimeter here or a centimeter there, Komlos gathered isolated data few people seemed interested in and interpreted it to make broad claims about a process that transformed Europe in the nineteenth century.

All the examples so far have presented historians who have reached out to other academic disciplines and incorporated rather surprising ideas into their historical analysis. In contrast, the remaining two examples come from nonhistorians—that is, individuals you would probably not expect to find employed in a history department. Yet it has often been said that scholars become so entrenched in their own ideas that only an outsider can suggest new paths and directions. Jared Diamond, at home in a geography department, and Jürgen Habermas, at home in a philosophy or sociology department, drew historians out of their comfort zone with their historical analyses. Before looking at their work in more detail, it is important to add that these outsiders depended on the work of historians for their conclusions; therefore, a real effective cooperation existed with historians.

Jared Diamond can be considered either an evolutionary biologist, professor of physiology, geographer, or historian. In the late 1990s he wrote *Guns, Germs, and Steel* to explore the fates of human societies across a span of more than 10,000 years. This popular bestseller was a natural history of the environment and a human history of societies in that environment. In examining the long history of human society, Diamond rejected genetic explanations of human success and infused his discussion with a level of geographic determinism— the idea that geography has a greater effect on human evolution than human decision making. This idea has become less popular among historians because it can be seen to belittle human achievements, but while Diamond recognized the dangers of overly deterministic explanations, he argued that a degree of determinism ultimately opens up new avenues for analysis.

Diamond invoked his determinism with respect to birds and land animals. He argued that the domestication of animals played a fundamental role in human development and gave a distinct advantage to societies with domesticated livestock—the Eurasian populations were the first to domesticate animals in an economically meaningful way and therefore had accelerated political and social development. The Eurasians did not, however, innovate cultural techniques to domesticate the animals. Rather, they lived in zones that had an abundance of mammals with domesticable features. To support this example, Diamond invoked the scientific characteristics of animals to explain why Eurasia had more domesticable mammals than either sub-Saharan Africa or Australia. Whereas the Eurasian continent had 72 mammalian candidates for domestication, the Australian continent only had 1, and sub-Saharan Africa had 51. Although the sub-Saharan continent had 51 species, none of the species were domesticated (in contrast to Eurasia, where 18 per cent of the species were domesticated).

A cultural historian would most likely examine human social practices to explain why the animals were domesticated, but Diamond, the evolutionary biologist, focused on the characteristics of the mammals themselves. Not all the mammalian candidates had personalities conducive to domestication. The grizzly bear and the African buffalo had headstrong personalities, and the African buffalo in particular was unpredictable and dangerous. Diamond offered other categories—diet, growth rate, problems of captive breeding—to indicate that the animal, not the human, determined the likelihood of domestication. Europeans were just lucky enough to live near easily domesticated animals.

To be sure, humans had the ability to move these animals around and this would, in turn, modify the cultural habits of the peoples who adopted them. The introduction of horses into North America affected practices of North American Aboriginals. While movie producers loved to create an image of a native tied to his horse, these horses were relative newcomers in the history of North America and were a byproduct of European travel rather than a function of long-standing indigenous culture. The woolen blankets associated with the Navajo people were made with wool from sheep that Europeans imported from another continent.

Geographic determinism can also be applied when looking at the migration of peoples. Echoing Darwinistic conclusions about the creatures on the Galapagos Islands, Diamond demonstrated how social and political habits depended on the physical environment. He focused on the Polynesian Islands in the Pacific Ocean because the inhabitants on these islands traced their genetic ancestors to the fishing and farming peoples who lived around the Bismarck Archipelago near Papua New Guinea. Around 1200 BCE the migration process began, and over the centuries descendants of the fishing and farming peoples found their way around the Pacific Ocean and settled on hundreds of islands. Because these islanders spread around the Pacific Ocean had the same ancestors, Diamond analyzed how the geographical terrain influenced social and political practices of each group.

The Moriori people, for instance, transformed their ancestral Polynesian practices and adapted to the environment of the Chatham Islands. Southeast of New Zealand, the islands were considerably colder than other Pacific landmasses, and therefore tropical crops had to be abandoned in favor of the practice of hunting the abundant birds and fish around the island. Importantly, the switch from farmer to hunter not only influenced the menu of the islanders, it had political and social ramifications as well. According to Diamond, they had little surplus production to support armies or more complex political organizations. Since their isolation precluded colonizing other islands, the inhabitants learned to coexist with each other. Thus the physical conditions of the island promoted a peaceful and pacifist culture that was ultimately vulnerable to attack from warlike cultures.

The Moriori were attacked toward the middle of the nineteenth century when the Maori from New Zealand raided the island and subjugated the local population. How was it possible that the Maori, who stemmed from the same fishers and farmers as the Moriori, were able to subdue their distant relatives on the Chatham Islands? Diamond found his answer in the geography of northern New Zealand. In contrast to the Moriori, the Maori had settled on arable land that sustained a larger population. Moreover, the Maori had constant internal struggles because the population density was much higher, which provoked regular skirmishes that in turn encouraged the development of improved military technologies.

Diamond has a scientific background and therefore placed scientific premises at the forefront of his investigation. Yet rather than presenting detailed scientific results, he synthesized the science to merge his expertise with historical inquiry. Diamond's analysis shows how evolutionary science pushes historical inquiry away from Eurocentric assumptions that situate innovation in the minds and actions of Europeans. Conversely, Diamond recognized his debt to historical inquiry, as his work leans extensively on the existing research of historians. Historians might balk at his notion of a historical science or the strong emphasis on geographic determinism, since it circumvents important historical questions relative to more recent history (How did the arrival of Europeans affect local culture? How did local populations resist colonization?). These issues notwithstanding, the outsider looking in can make the insiders rethink common hypotheses.

Diamond is not the only outsider to influence historical inquiry. Jürgen Habermas, a political philosopher of world renown, wrote *The Structural Transformation of the Public Sphere* in the early 1960s, and it emerged as one of the most influential works in political philosophy in the second half of the twentieth century. In a nutshell, Habermas argued that political stability in a democracy was only secure if citizens were active in organizations independent of parliaments and congresses so that the parliaments and congresses would feel continual pressure to respect the views of external groups. Since its inception the thesis has been criticized, modified, bowdlerized, transmogrified, decentralized, ripped to pieces, and then put right back together again. As a result, it has impacted historians who have focused on matters as varied as volunteer associations in England or public protests in India.

In a broad sweep, Habermas looked at forms of nongovernmental activity from the seventeenth through to the early twentieth century. The work has numerous historical examples, but two phenomena at the start of the eighteenth century were of special interest. First, he looked at the growth of a newspaper culture, because it inspired public debates independent of the state. Second, he promoted the importance of coffee shops, where citizens met in a public space to discuss contemporary concerns.

In modern times, when we hear the term "coffee shops," we might think of Starbucks or Peet's or the little café at the corner of Divisadero and Haight. But how can one possibly philosophize the café latte into something more than a tasty drink? Habermas presented the coffee shop as a unique establishment because it represented a locale independent of all external authorities, where citizens from all social backgrounds could meet without the alcoholic temptations of a public house. These conditions encouraged like-minded citizens to debate, exchange news and information, and develop into rational citizens who did more than parrot the views of the state. The British magazine *Tatler* was intimately connected with coffee houses and published articles that encouraged self-reflection (even if the magazine did focus on gossip). In the early eighteenth century at least 3,000 coffee shops already existed in London. As coffee became a popular import and spread throughout Europe, coffee houses multiplied and established themselves—in a looser formulation than Habermas would allow—as bastions of democratic sentiment in a world of kings and queens.

In this discussion on interdisciplinarity and professional cooperation, it is important to note that Habermas drew much of his information from a German historian who, in the 1920s, wrote about the role of English coffee houses as meeting points for the English literary elite. Habermas extrapolated from the work of this historian and invested the coffee house with its meaning as a site of rational debate. This borrowing of ideas is part of academic practice, but it has an ironic aspect to it. Although Habermas extensively referenced the works of historians and has even been criticized for doing no primary source research, historians are more likely to footnote Habermas the philosopher than the historians who Habermas quoted. In this case, interdisciplinarity has gone full circle.

Historians have criticized Habermas for exaggerating the sobriety of these locales, for some coffee shops did serve alcohol and were frequented by prostitutes. In the grander scheme of things, this historical shortcoming was not overly significant because the emphasis on the coffee house was designed to influence political philosophy. As a political philosopher, Habermas was writing for individuals who wanted to build political systems resistant to the authoritarian forms of government that had dominated Europe in the 1920s and 1930s. Habermas was suggesting that to prevent the rise of Hitlers and Mussolinis, two dictators who came to power by manipulating a weak parliamentary system, philosophers should look beyond traditional political institutions and find other places where citizens debated, discussed, and undertook activities independent of the state—only these sites had the strength to challenge the state.

In the early eighteenth century, the coffee shop fit the bill, whereas in the twentieth century larger organizations were and are still today required to keep democratic states honest. In practice, these ideas translate into the activities of nongovernmental organizations such as Greenpeace, Doctors Without Borders, parent–teacher associations, and so on. All these Western organizations are well known for challenging modern bureaucracies. The idea also gained saliency in post-communist Eastern Europe. When the Iron Curtain fell in the late 1980s, Habermas's ideas were deeply influential because they emphasized an active and participatory citizenry in all aspects of life. After decades of passiveness under communist-run dictatorships, Habermas gave hope that an active and independent citizenry could prevent the re-emergence of another communist regime. In effect, Habermas had taken the works of historians to create a political philosophy for the end of the second millennium.

But then the idea bounced right back into historical circles. In response to Habermas, a younger generation of historians repositioned their focus away from traditional parliamentary debates and scoured archives and newspapers for evidence of proactive citizens in volunteer organizations, public meeting places, and any possible venue that gave citizens a voice. Historians who were barely interested in coffee houses (though they might be Starbucks regulars) were inspired by Habermas's philosophical ideas to seek examples of the coffee house phenomenon or what has come to be known as the *public sphere*. Historians filled the shelves of libraries in the 1990s with studies on cycling, temperance, and educated scientific associations at the end of the nineteenth century. These new interpretations did not go unchallenged, and historians have adjusted Habermas's theory as they went along, but a philosophical idea contributed to the reinterpretation of the past. The philosopher borrowed from the historian who then borrowed from the philosopher.

From the central point of the historian, we have branched out into six different directions. These are effectively six spokes in a wheel that has many spokes, thus they by no means limit the choices available to the historian. They do, however, add further complexity to the job of the historian. While it originally appeared sufficient to get a handle on the facts, now historians strive to understand musical notation, mathematical formulae, medical terminology, geography, and philosophy. Of course, as the historian extends her interest into these domains, she risks becoming a dabbler who knows a little math and a little geography but nothing too substantial.

While this represents a real risk to the historian, it should not be seen as an impediment to exploration or as an excuse to block a curiosity that extends into nontraditional domains. A historian does not have to become a concert pianist to engage effectively with music, nor does the reader of Schorske have to understand musical notation to grasp the historical interpretation. Similarly, a reader of McNeill can do without medical expertise to understand how McNeill's interest in medicine allowed him to undermine Spanish claims about their inherent superiority. For if we read other scholars' works with a cautious and curious eye, we gain a much wider community of researchers. And if historians show themselves to be open to other disciplines, other disciplines will become more open to historians.

Chapter 4

THE HISTORIAN IN THE
DIGITAL AGE

All the preceding chapters have presented the historian in as many diverse ways as possible; whenever a challenge arises, the historian has to innovate new search strategies or consult experts in other fields. With such an emphasis on professional interactions, the discussion now turns to an inanimate partner—technology. Long ago technology began influencing the historical profession when historians like John Komlos realized that computers could sort through massive amounts of data. The digital age, however, has added so many degrees of complexity to historical inquiry it is hard to imagine how one might summarize its influence. On a day-to-day level, access to digital databases and online depositories has changed the routine practices of the historian; it would be interesting to see how often a historian actually visits the physical space of the library today. Now that archival film footage is readily available on commercial sites like YouTube, historians cannot bypass this information. YouTube will never replace archives or undermine the significance of textual research, but it is already an essential tool with a treasure trove of historical imagery. In line with the searches on YouTube, historians are becoming increasingly dependent on the algorithms of search engines designed in Silicon Valley. And archives and libraries are increasing their digital presence, too. In one search, I discovered that Harvard had digitized an early nineteenth-century journal from the Russian Academy of Sciences in St. Petersburg; immediately I had access to a Russian discussion on the invention of photography in Paris. The historian can celebrate the digital age as much as the general public.

The digital age, however, creates a whole new set of questions and steers research in new ways. For the contemporary historian, navigating digital resources can be extremely frustrating despite the gains; digital resources run in the infinite and therefore require refined search methods. In the future, historians will have to deal with servers that hold incomprehensibly large amounts of data representing every possible style of source. New strategies will have to be developed, and young historians will have to learn new methodologies that differ from those that were taught in the second half of the twentieth century.

A historian is poorly equipped to discuss the future, but research in the digital age requires a little prognostication. This chapter is therefore divided into two parts, the first on more solid ground than the second. Initially, we look at existing digital archives and materials that are already available for research purposes. The Open Society Archives at Central European University in Budapest has digitized thousands of documents from Radio Free Europe, the influential radio station that broadcast Western mores beyond the Iron Curtain. Since these words are being typed during the centenary of the outbreak of World War I, we also take a brief look at an archive dedicated to this conflict. The second part looks at how a historian in the future will access materials from 2015. Will our digital data be readable by future generations? How might they interpret the information they do manage to secure? Through what new channels, public or private, will they have to access this information?

After World War II and the onset of the Cold War, the American government wanted to influence the minds of Eastern European citizens. Since the early 1950s, millions of communist citizens listened to Radio Free Europe and Radio Liberty broadcasts, emanating from Portugal and Germany, to catch the voices of émigrés who had little common cause with the communist regimes. The station broadcast news programs, music, and whatever else the American authorities could transmit to deflate local communist propaganda. The radio station not only broadcast a signal, it also collected an enormous amount of information with its interviews of travelers to the region and its situation reports. The OSA, based in Budapest and uninterested in seeing the return of a communist dictatorship, has established a website where researchers can access tens of thousands of these reports.

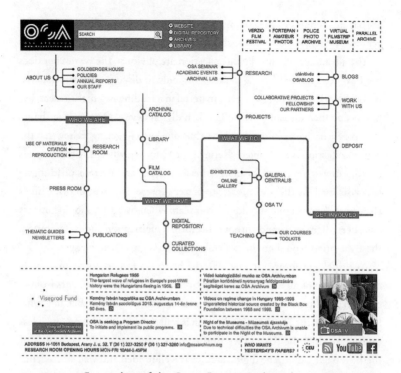

FIGURE 4.1: Screenshot of the Open Society Archives homepage in 2015 (www.osaarchivum.org). The webpage was undergoing redesign in early 2016. *Copyright the Open Society Archives at Central European University.*

Anyone who types www.osaarchivum.org into his browser will be taken to the website from whence he can begin his search. When you look into the digital repository, thousands upon thousands of scanned documents, films, and television broadcasts have been made available. The image above gives an example of the webpage.

In a search box, the user can type in terms and get results according to the keywords the archivists have selected (keyword searches do not scour the content of documents). The search can also be fine-tuned according to language, region, genre, year, and so on. If successful, the search will provide several options that the user can click on to access the complete document. For example, if one searches for "Sweden," the search engine gives 4,346 returns. One document describes the experience of a Polish nurse who arrived as a refugee in Sweden. Presented in four pages, the positive story confronted the propaganda efforts of the communist regimes to depict the horrors of refugees in Sweden. All of these documents can be easily downloaded.

The advantages of this digital collection are obvious. The researcher does not have to travel to physical depositories only to discover that the material is not there. Instead of reading the material in a reading room, the researcher has a copy that she can place on her own digital device. On the other hand, the process of digitization takes time, thus one has a lingering feeling that the digital collection is incomplete. Returns for Hungary, where the collection is based, outweigh returns for most other countries, and periods of Hungarian crisis, such as the mid-1950s, are better represented than difficult times elsewhere. And yet one should not complain when over 100,000 documents have been digitized—and without this formal digitization and classification, these materials would not be available through regular search engines.

At http://europeana1914-1918.eu, the historian has access to an entirely different form of digital archive. With over 400,000 rare documents from 12 countries and tens of thousands of contributions from the public in countless languages, the Europeana collection is much more eclectic and much less centralized than the Radio Free Europe collection. As an official project of the European Union, the digital archive is well funded and well steered, but it lacks the easy access of the Radio Free Europe collection precisely because it is so vast and contains so much ephemera. Users can choose to search the records of official institutions affiliated with the project or public records submitted to the project or both. Because the website aggregates materials from various institutions, the materials are presented according to the preservation practices of each institution and the archival practices unique to each individual country. Diaries, the backs of postcards, and instruction manuals have been scanned in different ways.

The digital archive makes access possible, but it is still difficult to determine what one is looking at or the context of the record. The vast number of postcards and personal photos hang in the air and thus present challenges of their own: How can a historian interpret a single comment on the back of a postcard? What can yet another photograph of a soldier in a small town tell us? Similarly, the search engines reveal the complexity of archival collections. A search for a French document can lead you to an Italian institution where it rests but gives little sense of whether similar documents exist in France.

These collections are invaluable even if they are works in progress. Historians have to work with technologies and leap into digital infinity even in less-than-ideal circumstances. It is hard to determine how quickly digital archives accelerate the research process, but they certainly give immediate access to enough documents to keep the historian busy even when not specifically on a research trip. We just hope that the increased availability of digital resources won't tie the historian to her desk and turn the roaming researcher into an office-bound web surfer.

Of course, future generations will encounter even more digital materials. To return to a statistic from the introduction of this book, if, as Google claims, more information is produced on the web every two days than what was produced from the beginning of time until the year 2003, then surely there will come a time when all the information from before 2003 can be neatly digitized. So will the historian of the future live in a completely digitized world? This is obviously not yet the case: Google Books lists innumerable titles without providing the complete digital content of the book. While the digitization of materials from before 2003 will be a boon to historians, historians of the future will also have to deal with all the sources that were born digitally. A century hence, the historian who assesses the Obama years in the United States will be sorting through the digital information produced after 2003. This begs the question: Where do I start? How do you find the needle in the haystack when the haystack is as large as planet Earth? If historians in the nineteenth century celebrated archives because they finally had access to ample documents, the historian of the future might curse the digital age.

The digitization of source material will certainly present new challenges. The next few pages look at some of these possible hurdles and assess strategies for the historian. How does one sift through and choose between sources that seem entirely random? How should a historian treat Internet sources that continue to change and are different depending on who is surfing the web? How can the historian guarantee access to old servers when we have no idea who will own those servers in the future? Finally, how dependent will the historian become on the technologies and the individuals who design those technologies?

We just have to imagine a historian 50 years from now surfing the web much like we do today. If researchers have the web equivalent of Apple's Time Machine, they can put in search terms and access pages of interest to social, economic, cultural, and political historians. If the historian wants to know what people felt while eating or drinking, she only has to access an archived server. For example, she might come across reviews about the Tattle Tale Room in Los Angeles, a bar that is reviewed on the Internet. She can read the opinions of essentially anonymous individuals. Here are two excerpts from the reviewers:

> Tattle Tale Room is disgusting. I like a good dive bar, and that's not an oxymoron. But this tavern is just awful. I saw a man throw up on the floor (no one else noticed—he was adept at public barfing). Then he came over and KISSED my visiting friend on the cheek. Welcome to America, darling. Here's a dose of class for you.

> It was pretty much dead when we were there, except for this nasty a** cougar that kept hitting on my friend. She looked like a Poison groupie or worse. She kept saying how young the both of us looked and how handsome we were. Please lady I'm trying to drink here and NO you can't take a sip out of my glass. Thankfully she left to go buy some cigarettes and never came back.

Millions, if not billions, of such excerpts already exist in digital form.

The excerpts may appear trivial, but they contain valuable information about social behavior. The authors hint at attitudes toward the aging process among women (cougars), means of expressing profanity without direct usage (a**), shifting currents in the music world (Poison groupie), and smoking and drinking patterns in public places. A conscientious historian would not draw conclusions based on these two single excerpts, but when woven together with an acceptable sampling from other sites the historian can amass considerable data, which historians of previous eras could only dream of finding.

Yet the mounting volume of evidence is becoming its own problem. In the past, fledgling historians were encouraged to develop a command of literature in their given field. This normally meant visiting a research library and reading a meaningful selection of books in that field. But what is a meaningful selection when databases of the world's libraries let the young historian search tens of millions of books? The historian is reading an ever-decreasing percentage of books that he knows exist (versus the blissful ignorance of a historian who understands that he has not read every book but is unaware exactly which books he has missed). Similarly, how can one present a synthesis of sources if the sources reach infinity?

A historian of the nineteenth century was more likely to bear the conviction that he could approach, if not necessarily achieve, a complete factual understanding of the past. Individual historians recognized they were only examining a fraction of the evidence—a social historian studying the working class paid less attention to the nobility. Nevertheless, historians still had the sense they were gathering additional evidence to create a fuller perspective on past events. After World War II, it slowly became accepted that, at best, we could know a heck of a lot about a small slice of the past. In conjunction with philosophers who argued that our knowledge of the world is largely underdetermined, historians understood that our knowledge of the past is necessarily underdetermined as well.

The Internet has changed these premises dramatically. If we accept the working assumption that the servers holding today's data will not evaporate into thin air, historians will have to satisfy themselves not with a slice or even a sliver of the past, but with the disconcerting feeling that the more access they have to sources the more fractioned and fragmentary their presentation of the past will become. We have access to a fantastic wealth of sources, but seen as a percentage our use of them is converging on zero per cent. This depressing thought won't discourage our interest in the past, but what can we expect when this flurry of information does become available?

Predictions are dangerous, but it cannot hurt to comment on possibilities. The excerpts from the Tattle Tale Room bar reviews suggest initial problems. The excerpts are a fragment of the information available on the webpage from which they were drawn; the cut and paste function employed to present them in this narrative cut the text from a much more diverse information environment. To analyze the text without the web environment is much like analyzing the behavior of a monkey in a laboratory that is far removed from the jungle. When one accesses the reviews, the website blinks, flashes, and presents the reader with an abundant amount of information tangentially related to the review but nevertheless an important component of the overall experience of reading the review. The advertising on the edges, the links to other restaurants, the map of the neighborhood, related videos, and photographs of revelers add a dynamic element to the primary source.

An integrated analysis of the source will require a mixture of specialists. With the increased role of visual data and its challenge to written sources, the historian can draw upon visual analysts for the photographs and videos.

A graphologist analyzed personality clues in handwriting in the pre-digital age, but without distinctive handwriting in typed messages visual clues need closer readings. There is no need to appeal to phrenologists who scientifically studied head formations or physiognomists who scientifically studied faces, but visual specialists can unlock spatial and temporal clues in imagery.

Reading a webpage in a holistic fashion represents a new version of an existing problem, and at times it might be sufficient to limit the analysis to the text with the understanding that it represents only a portion of available material. An individual who read a newspaper on a Sunday morning in 1950 read the paper in a substantially different manner from the historian who refers to that same newspaper today. Whereas that subscriber leafed through whole pages of the newspaper, absorbing advertising and commentaries, a historian often accesses a digital copy not of the entire newspaper but of a single article within the newspaper. The database provides a cutout of the article much like what you would expect to find in a family scrapbook. Few people complain about using sources in this manner, though one has to be aware that the source has been decontextualized from its original content.

The digital content of a webpage is more dynamic because the content continues to change—thus the added urgency to treat the source as a whole. By its nature, the primary source is interactive in a way that traditional sources are not, and this interactive component is not always uniform. First, the continued addition of reviews and photographs shifts the content of the page; the page can grow indefinitely in content. The visitor to the page can also adapt the page to fit her preferences. Whereas the historian may be tempted to scroll through all the comments, a potential client may simply read the first few commentaries. This act does not change the basics of the source, for it parallels a newspaper reader who does not necessarily read all sections of the newspaper even if that information is fixed. A potential client of the Tattle Tale Room can, however, click on a map and zoom in or out to shift her understanding of the bar's location within greater Los Angeles; her reading of the bar will depend on how she situates it geographically. The viewer can click on specific photographs and evaluate the commentaries of others.

The interactive component of a website comes from all directions since the content of the webpage is tailored to what the Internet knows about the user. Two users can read the review of a Los Angeles bar on the exact same website, yet the content offered to both individuals can differ substantially because advertising and imagery is customized to the Internet habits of the individual. The specific viewer does not need to know how her page differs from the friend she plans to visit the bar with, but the historian will be faced with the conundrum that he cannot be sure that the source he has before him was unique for all readers; the source mutates into different forms. Despite the complexity of the bar review, this only scrapes the surface of this problem, since even more complex websites exist. Radio stations have podcasts, the NFL has automatic video advertising with sound, real estate agents add music to their websites, and yoga instructors can combine soothing natural sounds with relaxing imagery. The sheer diversity is stunning.

Two other aspects can be noted. The first is the unlimited availability of public information that is produced each day. In the past, a historian might have had difficulty tracing the activities of a private company because it guarded its own records. The historian only had access to the history of the private company through state archives, trade newspapers, or special permissions. Now private companies cultivate public images on their websites, and the changing face of these websites give historians clues about, if not complete access to, private enterprises. A historian of sports has access to league documentation, and a historian interested in social issues has immediate access to the websites of smaller organizations since volunteer groups now post regularly. In the past this information was hidden in unknown locations or, more importantly, not even produced at all. And even given this access, all sorts of information still remains hidden on private corporate servers.

Because it will become increasingly difficult for a single individual to develop a synthesis of the plethora of information available, collaboration among historians will become much more important. Historians already share ideas with each other, and publishers issue collections of related essays, but the vast amounts of materials will make co-authorship much more important. In a fashion familiar to scientists who work together in a laboratory and publish together in a journal, historians will cooperate at this level. Co-authorship will not have to be between two historians, for it can involve other specialists as well. Co-authorship will function much like the locomotives strung together to pull heavy loads across the Rocky Mountains. Even if the problems and methodologies are vastly different, co-authorship brings the historian closer to the world of science.

In these circumstances, archival practices will have to consider the complexity of preserving and physically locating the digital data, though users might never know where the physical data are actually preserved. Many historians today employ the Internet frequently but do not understand the science behind it, thus they depend on other experts to preserve the websites they will later need. The process has parallels in the pre-digital age. If the US Department of State did not have a policy for preserving documents, historians would never have been able to read the decisions and discussions of former Secretaries of State and the commissions in which they participated. Likewise, historians will not be the people controlling the servers in the server farms in the future.

The archiving of Internet documents is neither a new phenomenon nor a new problem; already in 1996 the Internet Archive (http://archive.org) began its efforts to prevent the vast amount of information on the web from disappearing into digital nothingness. Other sites provide historical snapshots of webpages so the viewer can compare web design over the past two decades and access some information without experiencing the dynamic content of the original webpage. Naturally, there are an increasing number of snapshots as the Internet age matures. Professional archivists are preoccupied with the question of meaningfully preserving this data. Does all data have to be preserved, or does the information regularly require a digital spring cleaning? Who pays for the maintenance of digital data (a cost that is often ignored because the Internet is considered a free resource)? In terms of storing digital information, the historian will no longer travel to government or personal archives but access massive amounts of information managed by private companies like Google. The extent to which Google can dominate the storing of information remains to be seen, but much of the new data generated will be housed in private servers rather than on public premises such as libraries or state archives. As server farms adopt archival roles, they might require high security to protect the information.

A controversy has already surfaced in France, where archivists are fighting the European Union to prevent the issuance of privacy laws adapted to the age of digital social media. The European Union wanted to take measures that would give Internet users the right to be forgotten—that is, to eliminate compromising digital traces of their personal lives. Members of the Association of French Archivists have argued that society has a right to keep a record of events even when specific individuals would prefer to wash things over or prevent the spread of damaging information that someone else posted online. The controversy involves state governments, private firms like Google, and the archivists who see themselves as the guardians of a community's past. The archivists want all information preserved but have agreed that, even in a digital age, not all the archival information should be made available to the public.

Services already exist to assist individuals in erasing harmful information from the Internet. But let us consider the more sinister case in which hackers digitally forge documents and establish a digital archive that only exists online. Fake documentation, forged art, and other forms of document manipulation have existed for centuries. There is no reason this will not continue in a digital format in the future. Forgers can add artifacts and data to the historical record that never existed at the time; it also stands to reason that digital forgeries will be produced on a mass scale. Photoshopped images, the modern way of airbrushing Stalin into a photo of Lenin, are already taken for granted. Two individuals who never stood side by side can be digitally "stitched" together. Computer scientists are already discussing ways to perform digital detection on images like the doctored one published in the *Los Angeles Times* in March 2003, in which a soldier urges an Iraqi citizen to take cover. To a certain degree, viewers have come to accept the ease with which photos are manipulated in family albums and in newspapers. But what about documents such as emails, tweets, texts, and newspaper articles? In the past researchers celebrated the discovery of lost manuscripts; in the future we may be faced with digital manuscripts that pop out of nowhere. With so much data left behind on old laptops and whatnot, such "discoveries" might be commonplace and leave a heavy burden on the individual who has to distinguish between the digitally real and the digitally forged.

Increasingly, historians will have to familiarize themselves with data management systems and understand the role of the hard sciences, such as mathematics, which create the algorithms that steer search engines. Historians once just relied on and cooperated with archivists and the techniques these professionals applied to the organization of materials. The organization of archives was rational and well thought out but did not involve the hidden mathematics that have started to dominate any search for information. Although the collaboration may not be explicit, since a historian may never meet a single mathematician, the algorithms behind search engines will dominate searches for material in archival collections. The historian will have to know how to reach into the deep abysses and dusty corners of digital archival material—it will not be sufficient to trust the first 10 returns on Google to find the necessary information. In response, mathematicians might well develop archival algorithms that understand how best to probe databases for historical information.

Looking ahead, it is still difficult to determine how the digital revolution will change historical research. From the pessimist's perspective, it has led to the closing of many bookstores where historians loved to browse. To the optimist, it has released scores of previously hidden or unknown information and created new professional challenges. In a more celebratory spirit, the ceramicist Nuala Creed was recently commissioned to create sculptures of the Internet archivists who are busily preserving all of this digital information. The figures can be seen on display at the Internet Archive's headquarters in San Francisco or as images on the web. (The viewer will have to judge for him or herself whether the online digital images are sufficient to grasp the artistic intention or if a trip to San Francisco is necessary after all.) There is no crystal ball to tell us which way digital research will go, but the digital trail is already much larger than the paper trail. It remains to be seen where the two trails intersect and what measures historians will take to accommodate this vast supply of new documents. In this sense, it is the optimists who are better prepared to adjust.

Chapter 5

THE SKILL SET OF
THE HISTORIAN

All the previous chapters have outlined dynamic aspects of the historical profession. But how do you train individuals to the point where they are full-fledged historians? What skills do they need and where does the training begin? The problem may seem mundane and merely pedagogical, but even a profession steeped in the past has to consider its future. In 2014 on *The Agenda*, a television program on a public network from Ontario, Canada, Steve Paikin invited panelists to discuss the role of historians and comment on the current attitudes of university students to the study of history—in a technological age accelerating into the future, is the past of any use? One panelist was a little shocked by the student who told her that he had no interest in World War II because it happened before his birth.

This is not the place to defend required historical knowledge, but it is the place to think about how to prepare a future generation of historians and to explore how a degree in history can prepare an individual in the broadest sense possible. Without suggesting a curriculum of courses that students should be required to take, we can nevertheless look at components of the educational process and explore historical pedagogy within the context of all the activities that have been mentioned in the previous chapters.

Since we have been exploring the historical profession in expansive terms, the education of the historian cannot be limited to history courses. Many college students have minors, so few individuals in the past 50 years have focused narrowly on history. There has been breadth for decades, but as the profession moves forward we should reconsider the necessary skills. Considering all the advances in technology, would it make sense for the future historian to invest a little more time into understanding those technologies, or will they forever remain tools we use but have little interest in understanding? These new possibilities lead the discussion into some career counseling. An underlying theme throughout these pages has been the cooperation of separate professional communities whose interests and skills frequently overlap. How can the education of the historian ensure that aspiring youth understand all the possibilities that are available to them? Since not every history major will write a dissertation and become a history professor, all career options have to be considered. We cannot forget our working title: *Who Is the Historian?* And we are answering that question with the understanding that the young historian can pick from hundreds of roads that lie before her. We just want to look down those roads a little and scout the terrain before we set out.

In the past we measured success through our ability to impart critical thinking to youth—if you can train the mind, you have trained the historian. But *critical thinking* as a term has lost its robust qualities because it is continuously repeated in almost all contexts. As a slogan, it has almost developed into a defensive term. Unsure of ourselves and desperate to protect our ever-diminishing territory in the face of technological juggernauts, historians fall back on the abstract qualities of critical thinking. If we can't develop iPhones and spaceships, at least we have minds that can cope with the complexity of the world we live in. It was Descartes in the seventeenth century and the Enlightenment in the eighteenth century that glorified thought and the capacities of the mind. In the eyes of Enlightenment philosophers, thought was the pinnacle of existence and the mind a heavens for humans. It was only in the twentieth century that the philosophy of mind ceded its throne to philosophies less concerned with the metaphysical properties of the brain. The philosophy of language in the tradition of Ludwig Wittgenstein or Jacques Derrida were untroubled by thought per se.

In this spirit we can shift our priorities from critical thinking to other qualities that better reflect the skills potential historians acquire. Instead of critical thinking, maybe we could talk about critical exploration because it embodies the features of former times without insisting upon thought. A critical exploration can embolden future historians to enrich book learning with contextual study and extend the parameters of history for life. Friedrich Nietzsche insisted that the study of history could not be an abstract, intellectual exercise but had to be attached to life itself. We can combine a remorseless interrogation with life itself and not just the texts we read. As Nietzsche, the Alpine walker, knew so well, the lived environment is an essential part of the exploration.

Within history departments the curriculum has already changed dramatically to integrate historical study with life itself. University course titles with geographical and chronological unity are slowly disappearing. "Tudor England," "Antebellum America," and "The French Revolution" no longer serve the educational needs of students. Despite word limits in course titles, historians have become more creative and pushed thematic issues of contemporary relevance into the forefront. "The French Revolution" may have been transformed into "Gender, Sex, and Revolution," whereas "Antebellum America" may have been transformed into "Race, Repression, and Modes of Resistance in Antebellum America." You can't judge a course by its cover, but these titles indicate a move away from chronological history and an embracing of thematic diversity. Thus a student enrolled in the last course will gain a basic understanding of Antebellum America but also expertise in modes of resistance that echo in colonial cases throughout the world. These issues are discussed in greater detail in Martha C. Nussbaum's book *Cultivating Humanity*, which defends both the classic education and its diversification.

An equally influential shift has taken place with respect to classes on the Western tradition. While these courses are still offered, they have been challenged by historians who teach world history in an effort to overcome Eurocentric interpretations of the history of non-European peoples. While an earlier generation thought we might lose a sense of our roots if we did not have Athenian democracy and the Roman Empire under our belts, professors today are more willing to situate students in a global context. This lack of attention to Western antiquity was supposedly part of the closing of the American mind, but after a long battle global history has emerged in a healthy and robust form. This movement presents global history in more dynamic terms. Instead of presenting China as a passive empire eagerly awaiting European innovations, historians of world history have stressed how Chinese demands had a major impact on the decision-making processes of Europeans. For example, whereas historians have traditionally suggested that the great Spanish explorers acted as they chose, newer arguments propose that the Chinese had such a thirst for silver the Spaniards simply satisfied that thirst—they were reacting rather than acting.

Developing courses on world history has been a challenge because it has the possibility of overwhelming both the professor and the student. How can anyone possibly cover all of world history in a 15-week semester? In the nineteenth century historians taught global history to their students but did so either on a country-by-country basis or for no other reason than to explain the rise of Europe. Nowadays, in the innovative training of the historian, the emphasis moves away from national histories that emphasize the strengths of one nation over the other; world history stresses the integration not separation of societies across vast distances. If Chinese demand for silver fueled Spanish ships travelling from the New World to China in the early modern age, then the Spanish economy in Europe was linked to economic demands in China. Their fates were intertwined. This new approach highlights interactions between states around the world.

Consequently, historians have studied empires in a different fashion. Instead of highlighting the glorious rise of European empires, students now learn about items of global trade. In the past, historians paid attention to the Europeans who controlled trade but ignored the social byproducts of this global network of ships. In a single semester the young historian learns about plantation practices in the Spice Islands and how the transportation of these spices fundamentally changed cultural habits in countries such as the Netherlands and England. Whereas traditionally these imperial powers were supposed to stand above the colonies, we are more willing to recognize that the colonies had a great influence in the metropolises. In England and Germany, curry-in-a-hurry and the currywurst have both culinary and academic value. In the process, history students are better prepared to live in the global village.

Another interesting byproduct of world history has been the emphasis on bodies of water. In the late nineteenth century and throughout the twentieth century, historians studied nation-states as discrete subjects of analysis. More recently, historians have experimented with bodies of water: What would happen if instead of studying India we studied the Indian Ocean? What if we studied the Black Sea instead of the Russian Empire? By sailing out of the harbor, so to speak, historians gain a radically different understanding of the world. Instead of focusing on how a single group cultivated its own identity, the water-based perspective emphasizes the interactions between groups with wildly diverse interests.

The Mediterranean Sea has frequently been studied for the nations that share a bit of its coastline. Constantinople and the Byzantine Empire, Venice as a powerful merchant republic in the Middle Ages, and the history of France on the Riviera in the last two centuries have fascinated historians. Although all these geographical areas lie on the Mediterranean Sea, activities on the land (leadership decisions, the economic consequences of tourism, etc.) have dominated the literature. Historians have, however, shifted their focus. In the eastern Mediterranean, historians have looked at Jewish, Muslim, and Christian merchants in a part of the sea that has been overlooked far too often. Detached from the geopolitical issues that dominate the land, interesting questions emerge about multiethnic and multireligious conflict in a space whose borders cannot be so easily defined. More attention has been paid to Greek merchants who developed a presence throughout the Mediterranean. In the seventeenth century, Christian and Muslim merchants could sail together in convoy (*in caravana*) to protect themselves against pirate attacks. These interactions did not always embody tolerance, but by analyzing both peaceful and aggressive exchanges the historian comes to terms with a world of continuous interactions.

If world history has a grand agenda, local history courses can combine intellectual pursuits with the physical environment. In the past, adventurous local courses were looked upon with disdain, for they supposedly lacked vigor because the library was not the focus of attention. Today the education of the historian can venture outside the library or the archive by heading off campus and into the streets of local neighborhoods. "A History of Walking" as an academic course would probably not have fit the parameters of classic critical thinking. Even if we generously link walking with ancient Greek Peripatetic philosophy, classic scholars would still expect the subject matter to remain in the classroom.

Nowadays, "A History of Walking" can easily split time between the classroom and the community and impart the skills necessary for critical explorations by walking through neighborhoods. In the classroom, students read, analyze, and comment on classic texts. To satisfy traditional requirements, students will still study Jean-Jacques Rousseau, the great eighteenth-century Genevan philosopher. However, instead of reading *The Social Contract*, students will read *Reveries of a Solitary Walker*. Walking can also be studied in an urban perspective. In the industrial environment of the nineteenth century, urban citizens gained leisure time and put on their boots to walk into the countryside. In the United States, John Muir undertook the great walks in the West and founded the Sierra Club, now one of the most important environmental organizations in the world and emblematic of a modern nongovernmental organization (NGO). Since NGOs have become linked with civil society and hence political philosophy, an exploration of Muir's writings on walks in the wilderness is also an exploration of political activism.

Walking with a class through a neighborhood is instrumental in arousing curiosity and planting a seed of exploration. Since a walk takes place in present time we might risk losing the historical parallel, but this is hardly a danger when walks and texts intersect. The act of looking at an urban map has parallels with archival research. The map reveals streets that will forever remain unknown, yet a careful selection of streets, much like a careful selection of documents, can reveal themes and cross-currents. In these circumstances, restricting the learning experience to within the four walls of a classroom has its drawbacks.

An outdoor walk in the city should not obscure the fact that students have long since been encouraged to walk as part of their curriculum. More often than not, however, these were indoor walks down the halls of a museum. Professors of art history in New York, Chicago, Paris, and Tokyo either took their classes to these grand museums or encouraged students to wander these vast halls to contemplate the great masters. It is hard to underestimate the emotional experience of standing in front of Picasso's *Demoiselles d'Avignon* at the Museum of Modern Art in New York. These walks through the quiet halls of museums complemented the book learning in the classroom.

While these walks still retain their importance, we can add another element of the experience for the education of the historian. When we visit museums, we tend to forget all the preparatory work behind the hanging of a painting. We read the short textual descriptions next to artworks without contemplating the skill set of the museum employee who wrote the text. So enamored are we with the Picasso, we wander off to see the

Klimt without realizing all the rewarding career possibilities hidden in the experience of visiting a museum. This is all to say that when the young historian visits a museum, he should do more than just seek inspiration from the art.

Museums, large and small, house professionals with unexpected skill sets. Curators may rarely gain fame, but they conceptualize how the viewer will see the art. If one looks closely at the labels, the visitor will discover that the art has arrived from collections around the world—if you ask, you might discover that a curator had to accompany a Rembrandt on a transatlantic FedEx cargo flight! Museums also need people with expertise to acquire and evaluate art as well as conservators who repair and prepare the art for display. Conservation is in itself a complex interaction of art, history, and science with its own dynamics and disagreements. When conservators intervene they are entering into a debate about changing the historical record— are we justified in stabilizing and restoring objects, or should we simply let the passage of time take its toll so that the aging process reflects the lived life of an object and not just its moment of birth? These questions belong on the historian's radar. Currently, they are more likely to be discussed in art institutes and academies, but the young historian should not shy from looking behind the scenes at museums.

The above examples focus on art museums because they gather in the spotlight in the popular imagination. They are not, however, the only institutions with historians. Natural history and marine museums have their share of scientists, but they also need individuals with historical training to contextualize materials. Individuals studying the history of science can branch out in this direction. Whether the work concerns the preservation of a steam engine from the eighteenth century or explaining how the social standing of scientists influenced the scientific experimentation with air pumps in the seventeenth century, these museums have room for historians. When bedazzled by the jelly fish at the Monterey Bay Aquarium, it is easy to forget that these institutions need environmental historians who can trace the swimming patterns of endangered and even extinct fish. Not all this work is independent of political leanings. Presidential libraries, which regularly hire interns from history departments, require caretakers who are sensitive and not opposed to the library's namesake.

Typically, the perception is that history may be lived outdoors but is learned indoors. Yet historians can find employment in a wide range of open-air museums. In the 1880s the Norwegians devised plans to erect a series of buildings to demonstrate the evolution of Norwegian building styles from the medieval period to the present. Upper Canada Village, located between Montreal and Toronto, re-creates the environment of a nineteenth-century settlement on the shores of Lake Ontario. On a warm day in the summer, visitors can wander down dusty lanes and eat bread baked in an old oven using the original recipe. If archivists are concerned about preserving correspondence and photographs, the curators of the open-air museum are concerned with the preservation of physical structures. The Danes have built a variation on this theme in Aarhus. The museum has created subsequent iterations of a typical city: Within a few paces you can be transformed from the 1800s into the 1920s and even the 1970s, where you can gaze through a shop window and ogle at the box televisions, cassette recorders, and cash registers.

In contrast to the stuffy museum of lore, open-air museums have been designed with tourists in mind. Yet they are not without interpretive controversy, and thus, even subconsciously, they confront each visitor with the process of critiquing the past. Historians are not trying to ruin the delight of the tourist, but as long as the museum is portraying the past and claiming to accurately transport its visitor in time, questions about the perspective from which the story is told arise.

The Ukrainian Cultural Heritage Village outside of Edmonton, Alberta, allows its visitors to "travel back in time" to relive the experience of Ukrainian settlers who built their futures on the Canadian prairies. The site has Orthodox churches of the Eastern Byzantine Rite to indicate that religious belief was exported across the ocean. But how can one integrate the history of the Jews who also emigrated into the story embedded in these churches? How can an open-air museum deal with a lingering anti-Semitism that was not left behind in East Central Europe? Is it worth burdening the visitor with such troubling thoughts when everyone is met by the smiles of young, costumed role-players who give the entire experience a realistic feel? Variations of this theme exist with respect to sites in the American south, where the perspective of the slave has often been overlooked in an effort to appeal to wealthy white tourists. These questions demand subtle analysis by historians who do more than just comb old cookbooks for bread recipes.

Opportunities for the historian arise when we look beyond the proverbial display cabinet. Institutions have websites that list the staff in each department. Instead of restricting searches to the collections catalogue, the young historian can search institutional websites and prepare visits to the cultural laboratories that exist behind the scenes.

Injecting all of this diversity into a curriculum might be an impossible task. If we continue the metaphor of walking in different directions, maybe we will lose our way, leave core values behind, and become fragmented. In his study of communal life in postwar America, Robert Putnam looked back with nostalgia at a time when everyone (apparently) watched *I Love Lucy*; because everyone watched the same show, Americans had a common subject of conversation. Now that we have hundreds of different television channels, the common ground has been lost.

A contemporary counterforce to fragmentation is, of course, the mass production of textbooks, which unifies readers and presents them with common discussion topics. These do not, however, necessarily encourage critical explorations. As more and more youngsters enroll at universities, the textbooks have developed into serious business. Authors can fund their research with well-received textbooks, and publishers have developed marketing strategies and combined online resources with the traditional physical book. These neatly packaged textbooks, with glossy photographs and exciting blurbs, make the subject matter more digestible for readers, but they can transform intellectual reading into entertainment. Instead of reading a pamphlet by Locke or a torn edition of the *Communist Manifesto* by Marx, textbooks present concisely summarized and sugar-coated excerpts to individuals. Textbooks offset fragmentation, but they come with their own disadvantages.

Textbooks are an even greater issue at the high school level because there is much less choice; entire school boards—even entire nations—select mandatory texts. In Texas, a controversy emerged because textbooks failed to recount the history of evolutionary thought. In this case, the history of science had been eliminated from the classroom. In the Russian Federation, where textbooks are issued nationally, the situation is of greater concern—how can one properly tell the history of Stalin to 15 year olds?

Controversially, the authors of the approved textbook did not offer a blanket condemnation of the ruthless dictator. Instead they condemned the violence of certain policies while applauding his drive for industrialization and foreign policy decisions. In the increasingly authoritarian environment of the Russian Federation, this decision has broader ramifications. Essentially, the history lesson is about contemporary political culture and defines the boundaries of acceptable behavior.

Someone has to make the above decisions and determine what version of history our high school students should be learning. No one plans to become a textbook evaluator, but in Russia and elsewhere in the world important state, national, and private commissions exist to decide on proper content. These commissions bring together politicians, librarians, historians, and others to make decisions. The membership of these commissions is highly political. In the case of Russia, the state is unlikely to invite a member with a less-than-patriotic worldview, preferring individuals who interpret Russian history much like President Putin. In less restrictive circumstances, these commissions bring together individuals with historical training to adjudicate important pedagogical issues. These commissions, when working effectively, can promote many diverse views and face the challenge of navigating between fragmentation and diversity in the contemporary world.

This dilemma has been noted for at least a generation in the academic community; long ago, gender studies very successfully broke away from the mainstream, and area studies programs have had similar successes in promoting diversity without fragmenting the academic community. The very existence of these varied fields has suggested that there is no single television show we should all watch and, more importantly, no single book we must all read. But even without a common background, the fragmentation is never that extreme. The historical past may be a little messier if we don't all draw from one textbook, but themes continue to overlap. In the same way the historian works in a professional web, different approaches of history overlap here and there; no two thematic approaches are entirely mutually exclusive. Instead of parroting the same books over and over again, the learned will engage in conversations and exchange experiences from various perspectives in a common, public sphere of discussion.

In an earlier chapter on sources, emphasis was placed on oral sources and the difficulties oral history had in establishing itself as a discipline—historians had a sense that it was too subjective and too parochial. In the meantime, however, oral history has developed into an important branch of study. In this vein, oral discussions belong in the education of the historian as a window to the past. Traditionally, the process of historical education involved extensive oral exchanges, but these conversations had a restricted listenership. The emphasis was placed on a group of intellectuals sitting in the modern equivalent of the agora and philosophizing out loud; Nietzsche did this with his friends. These conversations still have exceptional value, especially with all the distractions of modern technologies, but they are not the only conversations scholars should have.

Young historians always have the option to talk with their elders about the hardships of war, race relations in America during the civil rights campaigns, or the benefits of communism under Leonid Brezhnev in the 1970s. In the more focused environment of historical education, we should seek out stories beyond the family circle and take this opportunity to converse with ethnic, racial, and social groups outside our own. If we grew up in the suburbs, it is less compelling to collect the stories about someone else's youth in the same suburb. If we make the effort to talk with immigrants about their experiences arriving in a new country, or if a young immigrant seeks out the perspective of a sixth-generation American, the conversations will develop interesting cross-currents. Students can decide to sit down with members of a religious congregation, business owners who were affected by the Los Angeles riots of the early 1990s, or members of a specific union and try to grasp the past through these often neglected voices. As oral historians have long since argued, the conversations are not designed to get a more objective view of the past but to change the meaning that past has for us today.

The selection of conversations outside the classroom can also be conducted in languages other than English. Since English dominates the Internet and the scientific and business worlds, it is all too easily assumed that second languages are redundant. Yet even today the majority of conversational interactions throughout the world are conducted in languages other than English. Moreover, we have a certain responsibility to learn local languages. On one of many walks through Los Angeles, I vividly remember walking into a store to purchase a bottle of Coke. As I approached the counter I heard the owner and another man speaking Spanish to each other. I had not uttered a word, but the moment I placed the Coke on the counter he switched to English and told me what it cost. As I left, I heard them switch right back into Spanish. I had a deep sense of unease because I felt like a tourist in my own city. Something was amiss.

One could hardly justify financing second-language education to purchase cola, but the story addresses inequities and opportunities. When we stick to our own language group, be it Spanish or English, we become entrenched in the same stories of that language group. On the other hand, the youth who venture into other language zones act as bridges between cultures. They have access to the printed record of these zones and can write, say, a history of religion in Los Angeles without ignoring the Latino contribution because they cannot read Spanish ecclesiastical records. Beyond the academic world, language skills are critical for integration with community organizations and community activists. A bilingual candidate as curator for an inner-city cultural organization is an ideal fit since language, as has long been emphasized, communicates cultural understanding. In fact, many bilingual children do not realize the gift they have.

All too often the linguistic component in the education of the historian is seen as a luxury. This obscures the importance languages can have in choosing one's career path. It is quite true that one can get by in English, but the education of the historian is not about getting by. Armed with French and English, the history major can aspire to become an ambassador, a cultural attaché, a specialist in international law in Paris, Montreal, Algiers, Beirut, and numerous other places around the world. With Chinese, a more difficult language for the English speaker to master, doors open throughout Asia, whether as a Greenpeace activist, a leader of a trade mission, or part of a human rights delegation. These future directions open roads for the history student even if they are not directly related to the facts of history.

In fields such as library or archival sciences, languages are centrally important. Major libraries have foreign language collections and catalogue books written in hundreds of languages and in scores of alphabets. Every major library has a team of librarians who have familiarity with translation.

Archives cannot predict what materials will be donated or unexpectedly located. These individuals may not have to read Dostoyevsky in Russian, but they do have to understand the general theme of the documents they receive in Russian. Importantly, proficiency in a language does not mean speaking it like a native; this would be setting the bar far too high. It means being able to navigate a language. For some, this will mean reading; for others, listening; and for others still, speaking. Whatever the level, linguistic proficiency is hardly something you can do without.

The perfection of second and third languages should not, however, replace training in the home language. All historians need to master language skills so they can clearly present their ideas in writing. The successful writer does not simply perfect English grammar. Rather, she develops a personal style that can convey complex ideas to a variety of audiences. Good historical writing has a rhythm that draws the reader along and avoids listing dates or seeking acclaim for presenting events in chronological order. The historian must explain the relationship between causes and consequences and weave together a complex narrative that explains this causality. In successful cases, the reader will navigate an analysis that incorporates theory, interpretation, and a wide range of primary sources. Rather than just assembling a heap of data about the Freemasons in seventeenth-century England, the careful historian links the data with theories of associational life, such as the ones mentioned earlier with Habermas, and can then ask grander questions about the development of democracy among broader swaths of the population: Does participation in an association mimic participation in a parliamentary setting and thus encourage democracy among its members? Does membership cause democratic sentiment? Is democracy a consequence of associational life? When these questions are answered in an effective narrative, they will have an impact on the reader. Clear prose is not the handmaiden of thought but an intricate part of the process at the end of which is an influential historical work. The careful writer is a careful thinker, and the careful thinker finds the most respect among her readers.

In the current atmosphere, history students also need scientific training. What is the place of technology in the curriculum of the historian? Often a student will major in history and then continue on to complete a Masters in library sciences or archival sciences. If the history major continues into a program with a science component, shouldn't there be preliminary preparation in the sciences themselves? In other words, should a history major have some mathematical preparation in the event these tools are necessary to be a librarian, an archivist, or even someone trained to create the databases we use to search for books? Universities offer math and computer courses as part of core curricula, but these are general courses and not specifically designed to help the historian who might end up in a library science program. How much math or computer programming does the modern historian need to know?

The answer lies in the fact that it is not how much we know, but that we know the right math or programming materials. In existing historical studies, historians have demonstrated knowledge in statistical methods and processed vast amounts of data with mathematical formulae. There should be some concern, as mentioned in Chapter 4, that mathematical algorithms are the main steering agents in our search for materials (and we are at risk of them becoming the sole steering agents in a digital universe). At universities with library science programs, similar courses exist. At the University of North Carolina, the School of Information and Library Science offers courses such as "Human-Computer Interaction," "Information Systems Analysis and Design," and "Information and Computer Ethics." With attention given to interfaces, these courses permit an exploration of how user interfaces influence the presentation of information. Although these courses are designed with library students in mind, they should be considered within the scope of the historian's education since they are intimately connected with the search for sources. They contain the necessary exposure to technological details without bogging down the historian.

At a time when the humanities are being overwhelmed by technology, introducing technology into the curriculum can be seen as waving the white flag. In isolation perhaps this is true, but within the context of all the possibilities mentioned in this chapter it is really no more than building on a solid foundation and admitting that the preparation of young historians is changing.

At a banal level, all the above comments reflect the winding path of life itself. More significantly, they re-situate the education of the historian so that it is not just seen as a straight line to the professoriate. Since few history majors become history professors, it is difficult to predict the trajectory they will choose. This being so, it is hard to justify preparing them for a trajectory they are highly unlikely to take.

The fragmentation and diversification of education has pushed the profession forward, but not in a traditional sense. Historians of the nineteenth century promoted the idea of progress. Hegel saw history moving forward on an inescapable path toward its culmination in the Prussian state. At the end of the nineteenth century, British historians envisioned progress in terms of the Empire and marveled at the steps forward their industrial nation had made. Of course, this idea of progress tended to ignore the fate of the less fortunate in Africa and India. Instead it focused on the advantages in the home country. As E.H. Carr wrote after World War II, progress for some is not progress for others. We now take this statement for granted when we look to the past. It can, however, resonate when considering the education of young historians—if we can no longer write with confidence about historical progress, can we still assert that the education of historians is progressing? If the study has become fragmented and education now pulls in all directions, hasn't progress been thrown out somewhere in an alley or on a side street? Not at all, for the study of history is making great strides if we just accept that progress means understanding the past in increasingly complex ways.

Over the years and with some resistance, the curriculum has been diversified to include the interests of groups that were traditionally overlooked. If the content inside the classroom has already changed dramatically, it should not be difficult to expand interest outside the classroom. The education of the historian is more than just a tidy prep school exercise or a component in the ambiguous notion of critical thinking. It has to respect the myriad career opportunities that exist on a planet with billions of people. Reading classical texts and reading extensively still remains at the core of the historical curriculum, but a transition has taken place. The traditional study of history needs to be complemented with the opportunities presented above.

The example of walking embodies this transition. If we limit the historical education to purely intellectual and contemplative exercises, then pacing slowly around the classroom is up to the task. If we put our feet to the ground and explore physical neighborhoods outside our campuses, our minds will be regenerated through the curiosity these rambles entail. We don't have to swagger or strut, since there is no rush to finish the walking route. We do, however, have to keep all our senses alert, as even the simplest map has thousands upon thousands of possible routes.

Chapter 6

HISTORY, THE HISTORIAN, AND THE HUMANITIES

A significant effort has been made to present the multifaceted aspects of the historical profession and the opportunities that spring from a historical education. The historian can travel the world in all sorts of guises and perform all sorts of work. The individual opportunities are immense but, in the current climate, does this still matter when paired against the possibilities in science or business? Are history graduates and their fellows in the humanities being swamped by the technologies around us? In a recent defense of the humanities, a columnist of the *New York Times* gave a brief indication of contributions from the humanities and lamented the social separation of the well-paid computer scientist and the frustrated dog walker who had received a degree in history or literature. Even the thought of the comparison is depressing.

This is not, however, the only starting point to justify history and similar endeavors. Instead of looking at the individual possibilities discussed in previous chapters, we can end by placing history in the largest framework possible, that of the humanities, and examine changes brought about when humans think of the world around them in a humanistic perspective. The dog walker may not have found fulfillment in the area for which he was trained, but he certainly read the works of historians and thinkers who fundamentally changed the world we live in. Where would the gay rights movement be without fundamental works by historically inclined thinkers such as Friedrich Nietzsche and Michel Foucault? Where would America be today without scholars who have invested decades in studying not only the injustices of racism but also the changing strategies of those in power to alienate minority groups? What would be the fate of our democracy if we did not have historians and philosophers who emphasized that democracy is not just a function of Congress or Parliament but of volunteer organizations throughout the world?

History has to be placed in this much larger framework because of the critical voices that have been raised across the academic and public spectrum. Although history and related pursuits have introduced fundamental changes in worldviews, they have been portrayed as an extravagance when set against more practical pursuits such as marketing, medical science, or engineering. Across the globe, scholars and students are reconsidering the role of the humanities in education at high school, in universities, and throughout the lives of citizens in democratic states. In extreme cases, scholars worry that an education in the humanities will go the way of the dodo bird. It must be admitted that, over the centuries, certain professions have gone extinct. We no longer have gaslighters, alchemists have disappeared, and phrenologists were, for good reason, put out of business long ago. The humanities, however, are about life itself and not just about the careers that make ends meet.

Defenders of the humanities have been around for a while. In the early 1870s Nietzsche criticized technical education as providing dead knowledge that was effectively useless; he criticized the German education system for creating automatons who could do little more than perform industrial tasks like engineering. This education did not add to the intrinsic value of being human, though it could build a speedier locomotive. German engineering pupils absorbed knowledge for no other reason than to perform a task. Our current system can be criticized for providing automatons for corporate America. Instead, Nietzsche volunteered "history for life" and a soul-searching education that probed deep into the human psyche and changed that psyche.

We need to finish this discussion by situating the historian within this fundamental network. The humanities appear to struggle because of a lack of recognition, but a careful approach to the problem can make sure we end on the optimistic note so characteristic of the last pages. A trinity of thought has always been popular, so let us divide the problem into three.

We will generally look at how the humanities have made massive changes both seen and unseen, and then look at how historians have played a role in the major arguments and events of the twentieth century. Finally, we will look at the overlap of the humanities and science so that they are viewed as working together. Science has an advantage because scientists are readily identifiable—when schoolchildren are asked to name the smartest person to have lived, they tend to answer Albert Einstein, whose last name has become an acceptable synonym for "brainy." Scientists receive more recognizable prizes for their efforts. The Nobel Prize, introduced at about the same time that Nietzsche was lamenting the predominance of the hard sciences, celebrates first and foremost the efforts of scientists. It is much more difficult to identify the humanists who have played an important role. As we shall see, though, they stand next to and not in the shadows of scientists.

There is no small irony in this because every day we are exposed to the humanities in ways that cannot be linked to an easily recognizable label or that do not have a set value attached to them. The value of the smartphone can be discussed at length because everywhere we look individuals hold these dazzling pieces of technology. While the little smartphone grabs attention, everything else in the visual field is a function of the influence of the humanities. If the holder of the smartphone is walking in modern urban space, that space has been defined by urban planners who have undergone an aesthetic education. Perhaps they have read the works of Walter Benjamin, who promoted the Parisian flâneur; or Mike Davis, who lambasted the urban space of Los Angeles; or even the Englishman Reyner Banham, who glorified the automobile in the same city. These names have not been pasted onto street signs, but the influences have left subtle markers all around. Urban planning, from green zones to soundscapes in hospitals to the transformation of inner-city neighborhoods, emerges from humanistic concerns. Understanding how human beings adjust to sight lines, how to attract diverse groups into specific areas, and how to provide family services requires more research than is involved in putting together the building materials for construction projects. Urban historians can highlight the successes and failures of green belts, the factors that influence shifting demographics in neighborhoods, and the attempts of socialist housing in the 1920s. Architects can build off these historical conclusions. With a better understanding of human sensitivities, these urban planners can create spaces that are more enjoyable to live in.

Of course planning can have a negative side, and here the lack of attention to aesthetic control comes at our own peril. By knowing so much about human beings, planners can create spaces that control human behavior even when the residents are unaware of this. The creation of highway routes determines how we drive; recent attempts to make Manhattan more pedestrian friendly have rerouted car traffic, thus drivers will be exposed to new street scenes. More ominously, planners can play music to control pedestrian patterns and influence specific demographics. Classical music can be played at train stations to keep away ruffians, whereas louder rock music can be played at restaurants to keep away older patrons who tend to linger and tip less. These strategies are not self-evident, but they emerge from innovators who have close ties to the liberal arts and the humanities.

We can also note where the impulse of the humanities is absent—where the hand of a liberal arts education could play a greater role in things we might not notice, such as the design of airports. At LAX in Los Angeles, one of the world's largest airports, the lack of aesthetic design impoverishes the environment. At Kloten Airport in Zurich, where the interior decorators have had their say, travelers feel more at ease with the gentle tones. The functional also comes into play with everyday corporate environments, such as a fast-food restaurant or a television station like the History Channel or even a textbook in an undergraduate course. These environments lull the user and provide a degree of satisfaction that requires little further investigation. The functionality encourages complacency and curtails a desire to explore. We become accustomed to the fact that a Starbucks in Los Angeles and a Starbucks in Moscow look identical, and we cease to question why two coffee shops, located thousands of miles apart, should look like twins. Somehow the environment tricks us into not asking questions or just asking the same questions over and over again.

These subtle little examples indicate what might be considered the hidden values of the humanities. In more obvious cases, the humanities have played a dramatic role. Perhaps the best example is the emphasis on relativism, the notion that knowledge is socially constructed. Relativism has its critics, and many commentators see it as bad philosophy, but it is impossible to deny the social and political consequences of a movement led by philosophers in France and promoted vigorously in the United States. If we accept that knowledge is socially constructed, then we have to rethink basic assumptions. For example, past generations claimed it was natural for a woman to stay at home because she was less rational than her male counterpart. This claim has no value in a relativist's system because the role of women depends on unique circumstances and not sweeping, universal assumptions. Similarly, homosexuality was often portrayed objectively as a scientific disease and an aberration from normal behavior. In a relativist world, normal behavior is not a standard for anything and therefore homosexuality cannot be portrayed as abnormal. These are only two examples, but over the past 50 years individuals with a background in the humanities have been fighting pitched battles to have these new values accepted. As a result of these battles, many of which are still ongoing, society has been fundamentally changed—the role of women and male attitudes to women in society today look nothing like they did in the 1950s, and the very idea that gay couples have the right to marry was unthinkable in the 1960s. Without the humanities, much of this would have remained the same.

In these debates, historians played their role. When it became clear that domestic standards for evaluating the role of women were unsatisfactory, historians joined the parade and headed to the archives to uncover examples of active women who influenced society in the nineteenth century and earlier. Instead of just reading the Napoleonic Code and accepting the submission of wives to their husbands, historians have found all sorts of ways to demonstrate the social, political, and economic role of women. Leo Tolstoy may be the Russian writer we know best, but now the contributions of his wife, Sophia, as an author in her own right are becoming more well known. Albert Einstein may be considered the smartest man to have ever lived, yet we now accept the helpful discussions he had with his wife, Mileva.

In a similar vein, recent historical research has recast how we think about the oppressed. Instead of presenting minority or underrepresented groups as passive targets of abuse, historians have demonstrated the intelligent strategies employed to undermine authority. Years ago, historians stopped writing about a mob that stormed the Bastille in Paris in 1789 and recognized that the individuals, intelligent in their own right, had well-articulated motives and desires. Colonial rebellions from the nineteenth century are no longer presented as irrational natives rising up against rational Europeans. These historical interpretations tie in with contemporary concerns and have forced politicians to rethink diplomacy in the developing world.

Of course this is not just an opportunity to praise the historians who have written lengthy books, but also to praise the readers. In classrooms across the United States and Canada, students read these books, draw values from them, and bring them into their own professional lives. A journalist who has studied the history of Russia and Ukraine is better served to report on the catastrophe around Donetsk. A news reporter who has read Kenneth Jackson's *Crabgrass Frontier* will have a better understanding of how American neighborhoods were racially segregated after World War II. In knowing how covenants and residential "gerrymandering" work, the reporter will understand contemporary racial problems within a longer time period. Economic policies from half a century ago still have a strong impact today. When a reporter is in a troubled neighborhood, the reporter will situate residents in a historical and social context, which demonstrates how past laws have had a negative impact on present lives.

The influence does not even have to be professional. In courses in political philosophy, students learn to understand democracy outside formal institutional parameters. Readers of Alexis de Tocqueville and Jürgen Habermas learn that volunteer associations and citizens' debates in coffee houses are as important as our elected officials. Transformed into practical action, these works encourage individuals to take an active role in public life long after they have stopped taking courses. These values manifest themselves in all the protest actions that occur in cities. Over the years the nature of protest has changed, but citizens need to learn the art of protesting and carve time out of their busy schedules to take an active role in public life. These values are continually promoted in the humanities education regardless of the ultimate profession of the individual. In a historical education, students are now exposed to countless works that emphasize how small-scale public organizations have had significant political impact over the years. Historical research that has found social cooperation in the past has emboldened today's grassroots activists.

The research has not gone unnoticed. In the last generation international nongovernmental organizations have proliferated around the world. While Greenpeace and Doctors Without Borders originated in Europe, they have branches around the world, and volunteers who arrive from abroad must understand the local culture while adhering to the international principles of the organization. Greenpeace Russia, with its base in Moscow, regularly finds itself at odds with the Kremlin. For many young Russians involved in the organization, they certainly learn how to protect forests but they also have the opportunity to mature as democratic citizens with each subsequent run-in with the state.

Once again, we might have a hard time making the connection between a history class and a Greenpeace volunteer extinguishing a forest fire south of Moscow. The connection is not direct, but it should not be difficult to discern. A significant number of volunteers in these organizations have training in history and the humanities; they have been schooled to think internationally and have therefore sought opportunities in international organizations. The status of Greenpeace in Russia is both a function of its environmental populism and an academic attention on NGOs as the workhorses of associational democracy.

We should not suggest that Greenpeace owes its existence to academic philosophy. On the contrary, Greenpeace emerged well before notions of civil society became popular in academic discourse. Nevertheless, an osmotic relationship exists between such an organization and academic work. Despite claims about the ivory tower, the academic world learns from lived experience and in turn influences decisions in the daily lives of citizens around the world.

In these cases, historians have an indirect influence on contemporary concerns. It does not always have to be this way. In a twist on the study of history, a recent generation of scholars has added a dimension by studying a period called "the present time." Henry Rousso, a French historian, has explored how the nature of historical inquiry changes when historical research enters into our current lives. In a classical nineteenth-century version of history, the past and the present were easily distinguishable because a dividing line separated the two. As an example, until recently World War II chronologically divided serious history from dabbling with contemporary events. Rousso, however, has argued that in light of major catastrophes like the Holocaust it makes little sense to insist upon this division. The Nazi atrocities are not just a thing of the past but a human episode that continually stirs debate as a contemporary issue. In this view, the past does not have to be completed and sealed in a document box before historians can study it.

This approach permits the historian to focus on oral histories from living people who experienced the events and therefore has immediate political outcomes. Rousso has argued that the method can have a much more immediate impact on current events, thus making the position of the historian more controversial. In the 1990s, the French National Railway (SNCF) contacted the Institut d'histoire du temps présent (IHTP—the Institute of Present History) and asked it to undertake an investigation into French deportation trains during World War II. The IHTP historian, Christian Bachelier, undertook the project but expanded it to investigate the basic strategies of the SNCF, including its relationship to the government and to the German occupation authorities. The report Bachelier published in 1998 answered larger political and economic questions, so the deportations became a single episode in a larger story. Since the report did not seek to point fingers at guilty parties, associations interested in uncovering crimes against humanity were dissatisfied and felt, in the words of Rousso, that historians "were hiding the truth." The historian cannot predict the effect of a report and has little control over how a report is employed in juridical instances. Instead the historian has to work together with industry officials, experts from the judiciary, and politicians.

Of course, the last case demonstrates how the historian can have a positive influence on contemporary affairs. The discussion is incomplete without mentioning the other side of historical research—that is, historians who have employed their expertise to promote morally suspect positions. On the darker side were those historians who promoted nationalism at the end of the nineteenth century. John Fiske, for example, embraced social Darwinism, which was popular at the time, and had a deeply racial view of history. He and like-minded historians (and there were many) used historical research to espouse a version of race relations that encouraged European and American imperialists in their ambitions. The absence of research or the unwillingness to write about certain topics can also amount to a degree of complicity. In the aftermath of World War II, numerous French historians were unwilling to explore the significance of Vichy France (the unoccupied, southern part of France during World War II) because it was an unsavory episode with disturbing stories of French complicity when only the Nazis were supposed to be blamed. With historians downplaying the story of Vichy France, French politicians and citizens could focus on more uplifting stories about the resistance and the liberation of Paris. Historians can therefore hide aspects of the past to help their contemporaries forget about unpleasant episodes.

The overlap between the past and the present and political changes is clearly evident with respect to the Cold War. While many Americans see the Cold War as a victory from the past, the former Soviet republics are busily rewriting their histories to prevent the re-emergence of another empire. A key strategy of totalitarian states was to manipulate the historical past; anxious citizens of the Soviet Union risked punishment if they made positive claims, no matter how trivial, about life before the revolution of 1917. To fight the manipulation of history and the risk of forgetting, citizen groups have been desperately trying to ensure the continued remembrance of Stalin's crimes and the mistreatment of dissidents throughout the Soviet era. The human rights organization known as Memorial in Moscow has published lists of names commemorating the oppressed. In Ukraine, historians have been busily promoting the history of the famine from the 1930s. Outside St. Michael's Monastery in Kiev, a display reminds tourists of the famine. All this historical work is targeted at Stalinist brutality from the 1930s, but it also bears a strong message about the dangers of being dependent on political decisions in Moscow rather than Kiev and contains a historical narrative built around the premise of an independent Ukraine.

In light of recent events in the Crimean Peninsula, this historical message has been increasingly important and plays a role in resolving serious geopolitical confrontations. On the one hand, Vladimir Putin addressed his constituents with words deeply embedded in history. His speechwriters, trained in a patriotic version of Russian history, wrote about the Russian conquest of the peninsula in the eighteenth century, the defense of the peninsula during the Crimean War in the middle of the nineteenth century, and Nikita Khrushchev's ill-conceived gift of the peninsula to Ukraine in the middle of the twentieth century.

In response, Western historians have been publishing extensive op-ed pieces that position Putin's claims against what Western historians know about the region. Timothy Snyder rejected Putin's references to World War II and highlighted the historical hypocrisy of calling the Ukrainian protesters fascists. In a piece published in the *New York Times*, Charles King contextualized the actions in the Crimea with the history of the Black Sea region.

A historical tug-of-war was developing around a contemporary political struggle. As long as politicians insist on drawing on the historical record, historians will be called upon to respond.

Timothy Snyder pointed out that the protesters in the Maidan in Kiev (the city's central square) came from every possible social and religious background and represented a very strong civil society. Snyder centers his democratic hopes in these citizen groups rather than in formal political institutions that had become corrupted. This remark about contemporary circumstances was embedded in thoughts about citizens in the past who mobilized to confront government structures. Whether at a march in Washington, in a militia in Montana, or among the Freemasons in eighteenth-century England, citizens have formed associations independent of the state to protect their particular interests. The study of history clears the way to measuring the potential of these groups and acting upon it by joining an association or entering the Maidan.

These contributions in books and in newspapers are not without repercussions because the historian can quickly become involved in an intellectual storm. In 2010 Snyder could open the *London Review of Books* to read what another historian thought of his book, *Bloodlands*. Whereas reading has been celebrated as a core component of the historian's trade, here Snyder needed to brace himself before reading a stinging critique of his own work. Richard J. Evans, a historian and expert on the Third Reich, took issue with the analysis of Snyder, who had just recently published a review of Evans's work in the *New York Review of Books*. Since the historical debate touched upon the planning of the Holocaust and the murder of millions, a high degree of intensity was to be expected. At an intellectual level, Evans opposed the manner in which *Bloodlands* focused on a strip of land (primarily Polish and Ukrainian) between Soviet Russia and Nazi Germany and thus ignored important developments within the belligerent countries. Moreover, Evans suggested that Snyder had not paid enough attention to the work of historians in the field and did not have a complete command of the historical literature on either country. The language used to convey these sentiments was less than friendly: "Snyder isn't seriously interested in explaining anything"; "the endless succession of short sentences hits us like a series of blows from a cudgel until eventually brain death sets in."

Most reviews are less biting, but this does not take away from the main point: Whenever a historian seeks to sway debate, other commentators have an opportunity to provide counterarguments, and sometimes those counterarguments can be considered attacks. As one commentator on the above debate noted, "The review by Richard J. Evans . . . may perhaps be described as the polemical equivalent of Operation Barbarossa" (the code name for the Nazi invasion of Soviet Russia). In this atmosphere, the historian requires courage and conviction with the knowledge that, despite intellectual opposition, he should stand firmly behind his ideas.

But even in these strained circumstances, the written contributions to newspapers and the readers who add comments to them online cultivate the democratic process—that is, the process of participation in democratic debate. They undermine the idea that the historian and the intellectual exist in an ivory tower, the classic pejorative metaphor of academic life. Ivory as a symbol of purity, as it appears in the Old Testament, could not be further from the working conditions of historians. Not only do historians actively participate in public discussions, but much contemporary historical research studies the work of communities and community activists.

The term *community* suggests a local dimension, but the humanities have been equally effective in cultivating an international and global outlook. In the eighteenth century the German philosopher Immanuel Kant embraced cosmopolitanism and saw all humans as rational citizens of the world. Although scholars have criticized his assumption that all citizens share the same rational goals, they have continued in his spirit. Internationalization means coming to terms with global diversity. This is not an opportunity to celebrate the fact that everyone has an iPhone or that global markets are completely interconnected, but instead it is a chance to explore interactions in which cultural and linguistic preferences intersect and overlap. The world historians of the previous chapter have played a crucial role in showing that these interactions have been around for centuries. They have also helped us accept the idea, for a long time foreign to many, that a global village should not just be seen as the final acceptance of European and American values. The sensitivity of the historian and humanist demonstrates that each nation and ethnic group has its own contribution to make. It is the responsibility of educated citizens to recognize and appreciate these contributions.

Although the humanities have had a massive influence in all the ways shown above, the hard sciences have a much easier time defending their interests and scientific successes. They are often, if mistakenly, presented as undermining the needs of the humanities—why should we care if the airport is poorly designed if the plane arrives on time? Of course, friction between the sciences and the humanities is not new. In the nineteenth century German scholars differentiated between the *Naturwissenschaften* and the *Geisteswissenschaften*, and this distinction endured for at least a century. The sciences were seen as objective and empirical, and the humanities were seen as subjective and abstract. In recent years, the distinction in academic circles has become less significant. The hard sciences have been softened and many historians have adopted quantitative reasoning in their analysis. Isaac Newton, for centuries the paragon of Western science, has been transformed through historical research. His deep admiration for alchemy was neglected in later centuries because it could not be reconciled with rational science. In the past 30 years, however, historians have paid greater attention to his alchemy. The University of Cambridge, through its digital library, has made Newton's notes on alchemy available to anyone with an Internet connection.

Historians of science have also introduced subjectivity into the aspirations of scientists. Science has presented itself as objective, but historians have demonstrated how the science underlying social Darwinism in the nineteenth century "objectively" oppressed people. Thomas Kuhn, for example, has demonstrated that a human measuring device like the thermometer gained as much interest as the external temperature itself. In conjunction with this thought, historians have placed science within a social context, demonstrating how the success of science depends on social conventions and the social classes to which scientists belonged. Science itself has also been integrated into the humanities. The history of medicine, the history of disease, bioethics, and related fields depend on knowledge from the sciences. With each advance in medicine, historical trends change and new moral questions emerge.

Historians have to continue to challenge objective science to everyone's benefit; science has a history of performing experiments on minority groups, and these cases are rarely examined by the scientists themselves. Historians have to revisit laboratory experiments to understand where the injustices lie. The controversial interaction of science and history emerges in the story of Henrietta Lacks. The cancerous cells of this African-American woman reproduced continuously and were therefore perfectly suited for cancer research. No one ever asked Lacks or her family for permission to commercialize the cells, seeing that African-Americans were marginalized in the 1950s. Only years later, after the civil rights movement and much historical research on the social consequences of medical research, did Lacks finally receive recognition. Responding to these issues requires an awareness of science in the humanities; the historian of medicine won't perform heart surgery but she needs to understand basic medical advancements to comment on broader issues such as health care and the social impact of patient rights.

Despite all these overlaps and intersections, long-standing prejudices endure. In many circles the sciences are the standard bearers and garner prestige at the expense of the humanities. All too often we hear about the successes of physicists and the elimination or curtailing of departments in the humanities. Enraptured by the technologies that surround us, both the contribution of the humanities and the extensive cooperation with science cease to be of interest. When we consider the American moon landing in 1969, we are apt to see it as a scientific accomplishment, a great step for mankind, if you will, rather than a competitive political strategy during the Cold War that promoted scientific research. Historians have a responsibility to cast the scientific achievement in a broader context.

We should not just emphasize historians entering into the world of scientists because it is equally valid to show movement in the other direction and listen to scientists with a humanitarian concern. Over a century ago Einstein formulated and published his theory of relativity, a thesis targeted at colleagues in the world of physics. Since Einstein set out to understand the physical world, he had little or no concern for human beings. Even in his famous train example, designed to explain the concept of relative frames of time reference, the human traveler on the train is but an explanatory vehicle, at best a sum of atomic particles. The voyager is not presented as a rational, emotional, and complex human being.

Years later, however, Einstein became concerned with the destructive potential of the atomic power that had been developed based on his physics. In an effort to stem the destruction of human life, he rallied his colleagues to warn the government of the United States about the dire need to ratify international agreements and prevent an international arms race. Although

Einstein was not attempting to rethink human interactions or assess cultural distinctions with respect to atomic energy, he spoke to the human side of physics in a way in which $E = mc^2$ clearly did not. Ever since, scientists and historians and activists have marched together to protest nuclear weapons. There is no reason the humanities and science cannot walk hand in hand. We need both.

At the same time, the differences should not be eliminated or erased. The humanities have a flexibility of purpose that transcends physical knowledge of the world. Wherever humans act, the humanities exert a massive influence. In law, in diplomacy, in our newspapers, in determining the viability of minimum wages, in designing street layouts, and in answering questions about how we live our lives, the humanities are there. All too often we associate the humanities with the development of the well-rounded person, an abstract ideal that probably does more harm than good to the reputation and success of the humanities. When limited to talk about the well-rounded person, the humanities comes across as a luxury in a practical world as well as something that people outside the humanities can't really latch on to. It is quite true that exposure to music, philosophy, literature, and history gives every individual a better sense of who they are and how they fit into the world, the world we inhabit as humans, but there is no reason to stop there.

The standards we use to determine our laws depend on the humanities. At one time, covenants across the United States limited where racial groups could live. As philosophers and historians challenged standard conceptions of race, it became apparent that these laws had to change. When our diplomats travel the world to mediate peace or encourage friendly trade relations, the best ones have an eye on local culture and local mores; the worst ones are those who close their eyes and rarely succeed and hurt the interests of their country. The *New York Times* (a little to the left on the political spectrum), the *Washington Post* (a little to the right on the political spectrum), and even the *Wall Street Journal* (a newspaper filled with numbers and statistics) would not represent different views if their editors and journalists had not been influenced by specific political philosophers, social economists, and historians while studying at college. Discussions on a minimum wage cannot succeed as a purely mathematical exercise; they necessarily have to consider the racial and ethnic groups that will be most affected, especially in a country such as the United States where race plays such a fundamental role. Many of us drive to work without even thinking about who determined the street layout, the multiple uses of our highways, or the colors that dot the landscape. While the urban environment contains elements of "beauty by mistake," as Milan Kundera would say, designers are choosing colors, curving roads, smoothing transitions, installing gardens on rooftops, and desperately trying to make our metropolises worth living in. And doesn't Apple always have an artist on board when it designs its products? Isn't this, after all, what makes Apple special? None of this would be possible if young people were not educated in the humanities.

With all of these grand designs, what is the specific place of history? Better said, what is the role of the historian? What is the place of that individual whose activities we have been exploring throughout these chapters? The historian won't be directly responsible for street design or foreign policy per se, but she is implicated and the voice of the historian whispers around so many tables where the past tense is being used. When we think of the rise of the Russian Federation and the return of Soviet values, we need to know how the collapse of the Soviet Union is affecting current policy. When we analyze the state of gender relations in our society, we require a basis for judging improvements that have been made over the last few generations.

Situations that require historical knowledge could be listed ad nauseam. But we have to end with an answer to the question with which we began. We did not ask "What is history?" Instead we asked "Who is the historian?" in order to get behind abstract analysis and explore the activities of the individual who can influence all the issues outlined above. It is easy to see how the humanities and the study of history can influence our daily lives in unsuspecting ways. It is less easy to envision how the historian goes about making this possible. Unless of course we've read the last 50,000 words!

So who then is the historian? Is there a single person who bears that name, or is there a little historian in all of us? Everyone has a little bit of the historical in him or her, but the historian described above has more training and spends more time exploring the past. This individual does not have to be described as a professional historian, have a doctorate, or work at a university, but she does have to spend part of her day contemplating the past. Whether an archivist, a librarian, or a history professor, this individual is a traveler and an explorer, an adventurer into unknown circumstances. The individual is a reader and a scourer and a translator and an interpreter. These historians are integrated into networks of professionals in which they share discoveries, build on each other's knowledge, and dismantle structures whose usefulness has passed. Believe it or not, they are also computer experts who habituate themselves to technological change and use technological tools to rethink past events. In the digital age, this historian is not afraid to confront massive amounts of information, analyze it, and present it to readers in such a way that it makes sense. Whether in a book, a magazine, or a film, the presentation of the information shifts the public's attitude of the past and sheds a unique light on contemporary events. Therefore, the historian who fits seamlessly into a global community also has a public role to play at home. This is all to say that the historian is more than just an individual who works tirelessly behind the scenes to produce pages and pages of typescript. You can't judge a book by its cover, and you hardly get to know the historian by reading the book. Yet by considering all the aspects presented above, we now have a much better sense of who that historian is.

FURTHER READING

Appleby, Joyce, Lynn Hunt, and Margaret Jacob. *Telling the Truth about History*. New York: Norton, 1994.

Beard, Charles. "That Noble Dream." *American Historical Review* 41, no. 1 (October 1935): 74–87. http://dx.doi.org/10.2307/1839356.

Bloch, Marc. *The Historian's Craft*. New York: Alfred A. Knopf, 1953.

Burke, Peter. *Eyewitnessing: The Uses of Images as Historical Evidence*. Ithaca, NY: Cornell University Press, 2001.

Carr, E.H. *What Is History?* London: Penguin Books, 1961.

Diamond, Jared. *Guns, Germs, and Steel*. New York: W.W. Norton, 1997.

Elton, G.R. *Return to Essentials: Some Reflections on the Present State of Historical Study*. Cambridge: Cambridge University Press, 1991. http://dx.doi.org/10.1017/CBO9781139170291.

Gaddis, John Lewis. *The Landscape of History: How Historians Map the Past*. Oxford: Oxford University Press, 2002.

Ginzburg, Carlo. *Clues, Myths, and the Historical Method*. Baltimore: Johns Hopkins University Press, 1989.

Grimsted, Patricia Kennedy, F.J. Hoogewoud, and F.C.J. Ketelaar. *Returned from Russia: Nazi Archival Plunder in Western Europe and Recent Restitution Issues*. Builth Wells, UK: Institute of Art and Law, 2007.

Habermas, Jürgen. *The Structural Transformation of the Public Sphere: An Inquiry into a Category of Bourgeois Society*. Translated by Thomas Burger with the assistance of Frederick Lawrence. Cambridge, MA: MIT Press, 1989.

Hobsbawm, E.J. *Primitive Rebels: Studies in Archaic Forms of Social Movement in the 19th and 20th Centuries.* New York: W.W. Norton, 1959.

Kelley, Donald R. *Frontiers of History: Historical Inquiry in the Twentieth Century.* New Haven, CT: Yale University Press, 2006. http://dx.doi.org/10.12987/yale/9780300120622.001.0001.

Komlos, John. *Nutrition and Economic Development in the Eighteenth-Century Habsburg Monarchy: An Anthropometric History.* Princeton, NJ: Princeton University Press, 1989. http://dx.doi.org/10.1515/9781400860388.

Lacey, Kate. *Feminine Frequencies: Gender, German Radio, and the Public Sphere, 1923–1945.* Ann Arbor: The University of Michigan Press, 1996.

McNeill, William H. *Plagues and Peoples.* New York: Anchor Books, 1998.

Moran, Bruce T. *Distilling Knowledge: Alchemy, Chemistry, and the Scientific Revolution.* Cambridge, MA: Harvard University Press, 2005.

Munslow, Alun. *Deconstructing History.* New York: Routledge, 2006.

Nussbaum, Martha Craven. *Cultivating Humanity: A Classical Defense of Reform in Liberal Education.* Cambridge, MA: Harvard University Press, 1997.

Orwell, George. "Politics and the English Language." In *The Orwell Reader: Fiction, Essays, and Reportage.* New York: Harcourt Brace Jovanovich, 1961.

Schorske, Carl E. *Fin-de-Siècle Vienna: Politics and Culture.* New York: Vintage Books, 1981.

Veyne, Paul. *Did the Greeks Believe Their Myths? An Essay on the Constitutive Imagination.* Translated by Paula Wissing. Chicago: Chicago University Press, 1988.